THE BEST OF CHILDREN'S MINISTRY

CRAFTS

110 TOTALLY AWESOME
CRAFTS FOR ALL AGES

children's
ministry
MAGAZINE

Group

Loveland, Colorado | www.group.com

Group resources actually work!

This Group resource helps you focus on **"The 1 Thing"**— a life-changing relationship with Jesus Christ. "The 1 Thing" incorporates our **R.E.A.L.** approach to ministry. It reinforces a growing friendship with Jesus, encourages long-term learning, and results in life transformation, because it's:

Relational
Learner-to-learner interaction enhances learning and builds Christian friendships.

Experiential
What learners experience through discussion and action sticks with them up to 9 times longer than what they simply hear or read.

Applicable
The aim of Christian education is to equip learners to be both hearers and doers of God's Word.

Learner-based
Learners understand and retain more when the learning process takes into consideration how they learn best.

THE BEST OF CHILDREN'S MINISTRY MAGAZINE CRAFTS
110 Totally Awesome Crafts for All Ages

Copyright © 2007 Group Publishing, Inc.
Visit our Web site: **www.group.com**

Credits

Editor: Laurie Copley

Quality Control Editor: Christine Yount Jones

Chief Creative Officer: Joani Schultz

Art Director: Josh Emrich

Print Production Artist: Julia Martin

Cover Art Director/Designer: Josh Emrich

Illustrator: Jan Knudson

Photography: Rodney Stewart

Production Manager: DeAnne Lear

Library of Congress Cataloging-in-Publication Data
The best of Children's ministry magazine : crafts.
p. cm.
Includes indexes.
ISBN-13: 978-0-7644-3439-6 (alk. paper)
1. Church work with children. 2. Christian education of children.
3. Handicraft. 4. Bible crafts.   I. Group Publishing. II. Children's ministry.
BV639.C4B47 2006
268'.432--dc22

                              2006024547

10 9 8 7 6 5 4 3 2 1   16 15 14 13 12 11 10 09 08 07
Printed in the United States of America.

THANKS TO OUR TALENTED AUTHORS!

Tracey Abney
Charlene Baker
Lynette Brown
Carolyn Caufman
Laurie Copley
Gay Correll
Mary J. Davis
Kelley Dean
Susan Dietrich
Kathleen Dowdy
Wave Dreher
Tom Fethe
Brooke Fisher
Joy Gerhart
Nanette Goings
Susan Grover
Debbie Gustafson
Sheila Halasz
Beverly Harman
Debbie Holford
Charlotte Inskeep
Ellen Javernick
Carmen Kamrath
Janel Kauffman
Andrea Kessler
Robyn Kundert
Betty Lentz
Nancy Lettardy
Neil MacQueen
Todd Medlin
Ruth Mooney

Judith Moy
Estha Murenbeeld
Amy Nappa
Cynthia Nelson
Wendy Nelson
Lori Niles
Debbie Trafton O'Neal
Leticia Parks
Terri Quillen
Jolene L. Roehlkepartain
Deborah Rowley
Tina Sagisi
RoseAnne Sather
Doris Schuchard
Beverly Schwind
Anabel Silveira
Julianne Winkler Smith
Sandy Spooner
Pat Sullivan
Sandra Thompson
Martha Turman
Mark von Ehrenkrook
Tina Vosberg
Joclyn Wampler
Gordon and Becki West
Terry Williams
Debbie Zachariah

CONTENTS

CONTENTS

CRAFTS FOR UPPER ELEMENTARY 101

INDEX 123

INTRODUCTION

It's been said that you just can't do children's ministry without crafts. We agree!

That's why we've taken 110 of the best craft ideas from Children's Ministry Magazine and put them all into one easy-to-use book. Gleaned from issues spanning the last 10 years, these creative crafts are not only fun, but also easy to do.

Children's ministry experts from all over the country have contributed these craft ideas, so we know they work. And each craft is illustrated, so you'll never have to guess the next step. The helpful indexes make it possible to search by the Scripture reference or the name of the craft, so finding the perfect craft will be a snap!

Use this collection of best craft ideas

• to find crafts for your next special event,

• to fill in the gaps of your curriculum,

• as an instant resource when you need an instant craft,

• as a resource to help volunteers in their planning, and

• as an emergency resource when you need a quick, creative idea.

Keep this book handy—you'll use it often! It's a craft lifesaver for Sunday school, children's church, midweek programs, vacation Bible school, and camps.

Now go get crafty!

CRAFTS FOR

ALL AGES

ANGEL POP ORNAMENTS

Kids can make these fun ornaments to set in their Christmas tree branches and then eat the candy after the holidays.

WHAT YOU'LL NEED:

You'll need a Tootsie Pops lollipop, 2 white facial tissues, white string, 6-inch square of yellow tissue paper, and gold tinsel stem for each ornament. You'll also need fine-tipped markers and glue.

FOR EXTRA IMPACT:

- Read aloud **Luke 2:8-14,** and let kids act out the story. Have kids take turns being shepherds and angels.

- Ask kids why they think the shepherds were afraid.

- Let kids take turns sharing about a time they were afraid and God comforted them.

DIRECTIONS

Have kids place the center of the white tissues over their Tootsie Pop, gather the tissues around the base of the candy, and tie with string. Then have kids scrunch the yellow tissue-paper square in the center, glue the center of the square to the back of the tissue-covered candy, and fan out the ends of the square to form the angel wings.

Have kids glue a small circle of gold tinsel stem to the top of the candy as a halo and decorate the angel's face with markers. Kids can tie string around the angel's "neck," forming a loop to use as a Christmas tree hanger.

ALLERGY ALERT

Be aware that some children have food allergies that can be dangerous. Know your children, and consult with parents about allergies their children may have. Also be sure to read food labels carefully as hidden ingredients can cause allergy-related problems.

ANIMAL ARKY

Kids learn about Noah's ark with this cooperative craft.

WHAT YOU'LL NEED:

You'll need two large boxes; butcher paper; cardboard; yellow and gray acrylic paint; yellow, pink, orange, and black poster board; white, yellow, orange, and black tempera paint; paintbrushes; orange construction paper; coat-hanger wire; hot glue gun; clear packaging tape; scissors; newspapers; and paint shirts.

FOR EXTRA IMPACT:

- Paraphrase **Genesis 6-9**.

- Let kids color a large box as an ark. Kids can act out the story of Noah and the flood.

DIRECTIONS

Cover your work area with newspapers, and give children paint shirts to wear. Help children paint and decorate the animals. Allow the animals to dry before moving them.

For the elephant—Cover the box with butcher paper by wrapping it like a present. Then paint the box with gray acrylic paint. Using sturdy cardboard, cut out one giant heart for the head and two medium-size hearts for the ears. Paint these gray. Cut out pink poster-board hearts for the inside of the ears. Using black poster board, cut out two black hearts for the eyes, a 10-inch tail, and 1-foot tusks. Cut out two 41x2x28-inch pieces of poster board for the trunk. Paint these gray. Then curve a coat-hanger wire and tape it between the two pieces so it'll appear that the trunk is curved. Tape the trunk pieces together. Glue all these items to the box and reinforce them with clear packaging tape.

For the giraffe—Cover the box with butcher paper. Then paint the box yellow. Roll a sheet of yellow poster board into a tube for the giraffe's neck, and tape it. Glue fringed orange construction paper to the giraffe's neck. Using sturdy cardboard, cut out one heart-shaped head, and paint it yellow. Cut out smaller poster-board hearts for the giraffe's ears, mouth, and eyes. Cut out its antlers and tail. Cut a "neck" hole in the cardboard box and insert the poster-board tube. Glue all these items to the box and reinforce them.

BABY MOSES BASKETS

Kids love making these edible treats as they learn about Moses.

WHAT YOU'LL NEED:

You'll need large biscuit shredded-wheat cereal, marshmallow creme, Nutella hazelnut spread, melted butter, mixing bowls, mixing spoons, wax paper, jelly beans, and red shoestring licorice.

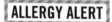

ALLERGY ALERT
See page 10.

FOR EXTRA IMPACT:

- Mix blue food coloring into marshmallow creme, and have kids each spread some on a paper plate. Place the basket on top of the blue marshmallow "water."

- Read aloud **Exodus 2:1-10** as kids eat their snacks.

- Read aloud **Mark 6:30-44.** Have kids make the baskets and fill them with Goldfish crackers and white jelly beans to represent Jesus feeding the 5,000.

DIRECTIONS

Have kids form groups of four and work together to make baskets. Have groups place 1 cup of crumbled shredded-wheat cereal in a bowl. In another bowl, they should stir 1 cup of marshmallow creme and 1 tablespoon of Nutella into 1½ tablespoons melted butter until the mixture becomes syrupy. Groups should pour the marshmallow mixture over the shredded-wheat cereal, and mix all the ingredients together.

Have kids form four balls of equal size from the mixture and place them on waxed paper. Have each child press a thumb into a ball to make a "basket." Kids can use a 3-inch piece of a red licorice whip to for a handle and attach it by sticking it into the top sides of the "basket." They should put a jelly bean in each basket to represent baby Moses.

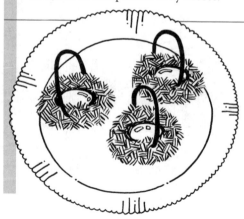

BALAAM'S DONKEY

Kids learn about Balaam's experience with these cute talking donkeys.

WHAT YOU'LL NEED:

You'll need brown paper lunch bags, pink tempera paint, construction paper, yarn, large wiggle eyes, scissors, glue, and miniature marshmallows.

FOR EXTRA IMPACT:

- Ask kids: Have you ever been scolded? How did you feel? How did the donkey's scolding help Balaam?

- Ask kids: Why does God want us to obey his commands?

- Read aloud **Colossians 3:20**. Ask kids why it pleases God when we obey our parents.

DIRECTIONS

Have kids cut the donkey's muzzle and ears from construction paper. They can use glue to attach wiggle eyes, muzzle, and ears to the paper bag. Kids should use yarn to make the donkey's reins and mane. Have them paint the inside of the donkey's "mouth" with pink tempera paint and glue on marshmallow teeth.

Read aloud **Numbers 22:21-34.** Then say: When Balaam's donkey wouldn't obey him because it saw the angel of God, Balaam became very angry and scolded it. When God let the donkey speak, it asked Balaam why he'd gotten so angry. Then God opened Balaam's eyes so he could see the angel standing in the way. Balaam finally understood why his donkey wouldn't obey him.

Ask: How do you think Balaam's donkey felt when it was being scolded? What did Balaam learn from his experience?

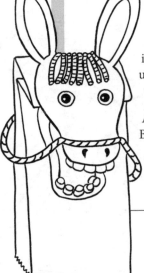

BEADED BOOKMARKS

Kids make festive bookmarks as a reminder of our different gifts.

WHAT YOU'LL NEED:

You'll need waxed jewelry cording, medium-size mixed glass beads, decorative card stock, hole punch, scissors, and decorative pens.

FOR EXTRA IMPACT:

- Read aloud **Romans 12:4-8,** and ask kids why God gives each of us different gifts. Ask: How should we use those gifts?

- Have kids find a partner and talk about their different gifts.

- Have kids write on an index card one gift they feel they have, then lay all the cards out on a table, and look at all the different gifts. Close in prayer, thanking God for the many gifts he gives us.

DIRECTIONS

Precut the jewelry cording to 12-inch lengths. Have kids cut a 1x2-inch section of card stock and punch a hole in one end. Kids can write, "'We all have different gifts, according to the grace given us'—Romans 12:6" on one side of the card stock. Have kids thread the card stock onto the cording as a gift tag.

Have kids tie a double knot 2 inches from each end of their piece of cording. Kids can choose any combination of beads they'd like and thread the beads onto both ends of the cording to the knots. Have kids tie off each end as close to the base of the beads as possible. Clip off any extra cording.

BERRY SPECIAL

Kids have fun creating this gift for people they love.

WHAT YOU'LL NEED:

You'll need red felt, green felt, medium hair clips, fine-tipped permanent markers, glue, scissors, instant-print camera, and enough instant-print film to take a photo of each child.

FOR EXTRA IMPACT:

- Ask kids: How can we make other people feel special? Why is it important to make others feel special?

- Let kids tell something special someone has done for them.

- Have kids sit in a circle and toss a ball back and forth while shouting, "You're berry special!" until the leader yells, "Stop." The child who catches the ball should say something special about the last child to throw the ball and then continue throwing the ball around the circle.

DIRECTIONS

Provide a strawberry pattern children can trace four times onto their red felt. As each child traces the strawberry shapes, take photos of the other children until you have a photo of everyone. Have children hold up a sign that says, "You're berry special!" as their photos are taken.

Have children glue two felt strawberries together covering one side of the hair clip between them. Then have kids repeat the procedure with the other side of the hair clip.

Have children cut out strawberry leaves from the green felt and glue them to the top of the strawberries. Clip each child's strawberry clip to his or her photo. Have children sign their names on the blank spaces under their photos.

BETHLEHEM STAR

Kids can use this easy-to-make craft as an ornament or gift.

WHAT YOU'LL NEED:

You'll need cardboard, scissors, yellow felt, glitter glue, and candy canes. Cut star patterns from cardboard.

FOR EXTRA IMPACT:

- Read aloud **Matthew 2:1-3, 7-12,** and ask kids why the Magi were so excited to see the star. Ask: How do you think you might've felt? Explain.

- Let kids decorate a classroom tree with their star ornaments.

- Let kids cover star-shaped cookies with yellow icing and top with sprinkles for a stellar snack.

ALLERGY ALERT

See page 10.

DIRECTIONS

Have kids trace the cardboard patterns onto yellow felt and cut out the stars. Fold the long piece along the dotted lines, and cut along the dotted lines. Weave the shorter piece through the slits in the long piece.

Have kids use glitter glue to decorate their star. Then lay the star flat to dry. Once the star is dry, stick a candy cane through its back to hang on a Christmas tree.

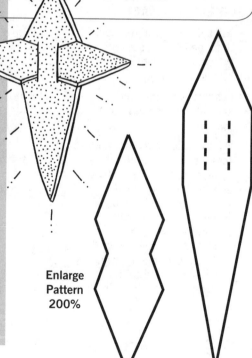

Enlarge Pattern 200%

BIG FISH SOCKS

Kids create colorful windsocks.

WHAT YOU'LL NEED:

You'll need colored tissue paper, construction paper, yarn, scissors, chenille wire, hole punch, glue, tape, and 2-foot-long dowel rods.

FOR EXTRA IMPACT:

- Bring in a fan, and let kids test their windsocks. If it's a windy day, take them outside.

- Read aloud **Psalm 8,** and ask kids why we praise the Lord.

- Have kids sit in a circle with their windsocks. Let kids stand up one at a time, name something they're thankful for, wave their windsock, and shout, "Lord you're the King!"

DIRECTIONS

Before kids arrive, draw a fish pattern to fit on a large sheet of tissue paper. Cut two tissue-paper fish for each child from the pattern. Mark the holes as shown on the pattern. Cut two construction paper fins for each child.

For each paper fish, have kids cover both sides of the mouth with clear tape to reinforce it, leaving the mouth open. Punch holes along the mouth.

Have kids glue one fin along the top edge of the fish body and one fin along the bottom edge. Glue the two fish together, leaving the mouth and tail area open to allow the windsock to fill with air and the air to escape out the tail.

When the glue is dry, weave one chenille wire in and out of the holes, forming a circle. Tie yarn through each hole. Tie the ends of the yarn together at one end of a wooden dowel, and glue them in place. Kids can carry their Big Fish Socks on a windy day.

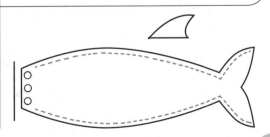

BIRDS DON'T WORRY

Kids make these fun edible bird nests.

WHAT YOU'LL NEED:

You'll need ½ cup marshmallow creme, 3 cups butterscotch morsels, 6 ounces chow mein noodles, 10-ounce bag of small marshmallows, and 1 bag of candy corn to make 12 to 15 bird nests. You'll also need a Bible, spoons, and wax paper.

ALLERGY ALERT
See page 10.

FOR EXTRA IMPACT:

- Teach kids this rhyme to help them remember **Matthew 6:25-26**:

  Don't worry about what you eat, drink, or wear.

  Trust in God like the birds of the air.

- Ask kids: How do you feel knowing you don't have to worry because you can trust God for all things? Explain.

- Close in prayer, and let each child thank God for one thing.

▶ DIRECTIONS

Over low heat, melt marshmallow creme and butterscotch morsels. Remove from heat, and let kids stir in marshmallows and chow mein noodles. Drop by large spoonfuls onto wax paper. Have kids use a spoon to indent the center to shape a nest. Then place three candy corns in each "nest" with the white tips pointing upward to represent beaks. Let cool.

As kids eat the "nests," have them talk about things they worry about. Assure them of God's provision and care for them by reminding them of **Matthew 6:25-26.** Explain that God takes care of the birds, and he'll take even more care of them.

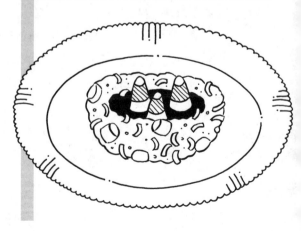

BLESSING BIRDS

Kids encourage one another with this fun craft.

WHAT YOU'LL NEED:

You'll need 1 pine cone, 1 brown pompom, 2 small wiggle eyes, and 7 precut construction paper feathers for each bird. You'll also need red and orange construction paper, markers, Elmer's School Glue, and scissors.

FOR EXTRA IMPACT:

- Read aloud **Philemon 1:4,** and encourage kids to pray for their friends every day.

- Have kids think of someone they're thankful for and tell ways that person makes them feel special.

- Teach kids this rhyming prayer:

  I remember my friends in my prayers each day,

  Thank you, God, for sending them my way.

DIRECTIONS

Have each child glue a brown pompom to the top of the small end of a pine cone. This is the turkey's head. Glue moveable craft eyes to the pompom head. Cut red construction paper to make the wattle and orange construction paper for the beak. Glue these onto the pompom head.

Have children each write their name on a feather, dab the bottom edge of the feather with glue, and insert it at the back of the pine-cone turkey and into its spines.

Have kids form a circle and pass their turkeys around it. When children get a turkey, have them create a feather with an affirming word about the turkey's owner. Then have them dab glue on the bottom edge of the feather and insert it into that child's turkey.

As turkeys dry, ask children to share some of the things they wrote about others. Close in prayer, thanking God for each child in your class.

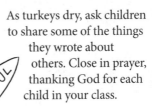

BUTTERFLY AND CROSS SALT-DOUGH ORNAMENTS

Kids love celebrating Easter with these festive ornaments.

WHAT YOU'LL NEED:

You'll need Ziploc bags, flour, salt, water, rolling pins, measuring cups, cross and butterfly cookie cutters, watercolors, paintbrushes, glue, sequins, buttons, glitter, yarn, a foil-covered cookie sheet, and an oven.

ALLERGY ALERT
See page 10.

FOR EXTRA IMPACT:

- Place dry ingredients in individual small Ziploc bags for easy use.

- Let kids make extra cross ornaments. Spread with vegetable shortening and cover with birdseed, then take home to hang in a tree for an Easter celebration the birds will love.

DIRECTIONS

Have kids form groups of four and decide which task they want to do, such as measure the flour, salt, or water or mix the dough. In a plastic Ziploc bag, mix 1 cup flour and 1 cup salt. Add ½ cup water, a little at a time. Squeeze the bag to mix thoroughly, then remove the dough, and form into a ball.

Divide the dough into four pieces. Knead each piece until smooth, then roll it out to about ¼-inch thick on a lightly floured surface. Cut with butterfly and cross cookie cutters. Make a small hole at the top of each cutout. Bake cutouts on a foil-covered cookie sheet at 325 degrees until golden brown, or air dry for 48 hours or until hard.

Paint the hardened cutouts with watercolors. Use white glue to decorate with sequins, buttons, and glitter. Thread yarn or ribbon through the hole at the top and hang.

Ask kids: Why do crosses and butterflies remind us of Easter? Why do we celebrate Easter? How does your family celebrate Easter?

BUTTERFLY WINGS

Kids learn that we are new creations in Christ.

WHAT YOU'LL NEED:

You'll need clear Con-Tact paper, masking tape, glitter, sequins, permanent marker, craft sticks, chenille wires, brown paper bags, scissors, and glue or tape.

FOR EXTRA IMPACT:

- Make butterfly-wing patterns out of cardboard or card stock for kids to trace on their Con-Tact paper.

- Read aloud **2 Corinthians 5:17,** and have kids tell what it means to be a new creation in Christ.

- Have kids remove their butterflies from their paper-bag cocoons and tell how that is or isn't like what happens to us when we become new creations in Christ.

DIRECTIONS

Peel the backing off the Con-Tact paper, and tape the edges to the table with the sticky side up for each child. Have kids decorate the sticky side of their Con-Tact paper with glitter and sequins. Then help kids lay a sticky piece of Con-Tact paper over their creations.

Have kids cut their Con-Tact paper creation into a butterfly shape. Glue a craft stick to the center of the butterfly for the body, and glue a chenille wire to the craft stick for the antennae.

Have kids put their butterflies into brown paper bags to resemble cocoons. Tell kids that a caterpillar lives its life on the ground and then makes a cocoon where it seems to die. But the caterpillar isn't dead; a miracle is happening in the cocoon, and the caterpillar is turning into a butterfly.

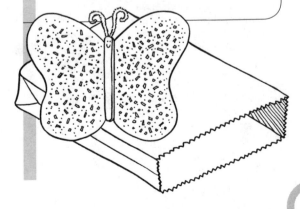

BUTTERMILK "MIRACLES"

Kids learn that miracles are possible with God.

WHAT YOU'LL NEED:

You'll need a Bible, buttermilk, 1-inch-wide sponge brushes, pastel construction paper, and colored chalk. Cover the table with a vinyl cloth, or have a sponge handy to wipe off the table when you're done with the craft.

See page 10.

FOR EXTRA IMPACT:

- Have kids tell about a miracle that happened to them or someone they know.

- Keep an ongoing prayer chart, and list kids' prayer requests for miracles. As the prayers are answered, mark them on the prayer chart as a visible reminder of God's power.

- Share a time with kids when God answered one of your prayer requests with a no. Reassure kids we can always trust God to answer our prayers according to his purposes.

DIRECTIONS

Read aloud **John 2:1-11.** Then have kids dip the sponge brushes in buttermilk and smear buttermilk on the construction paper. Make sure children cover the entire page.

Next have kids draw a picture with the colored chalk directly onto the wet buttermilk surface. The buttermilk will keep the chalk drawing from smearing or smudging. Set aside to dry.

Ask: Did you think you would be able to draw on the wet buttermilk? Why or why not? Did the people at the wedding believe that Jesus could turn water into wine? Why or why not? What is a miracle?

Say: God can work miracles in your life even when it seems impossible. What are some miracles we need to ask God to do in our lives?

Close in prayer, asking God to work a miracle in the areas children mention.

CATERPILLAR TO BUTTERFLY MOBILES

Kids make colorful mobiles to remind them of the way God transforms us.

WHAT YOU'LL NEED:

You'll need 2 wooden-doll pins for each child, tempera paint, tissue paper, glitter, glue, scissors, chenille craft wire, yarn, and pencils.

FOR EXTRA IMPACT:

- Bring in actual cocoons and butterflies or photographs for kids to see.

- Read aloud **Mark 16:4-8,** and ask: How is Jesus' resurrection like or unlike the butterflies?

DIRECTIONS

For the caterpillar, cut one chenille wire into thirds. Have kids form legs by folding each third into a U-shape. Bend the tips out for feet. Arrange the legs between the prongs of one doll pin, and secure them with dots of glue. Decorate the caterpillar with tempera paint and chenille-wire antennae.

For the butterfly, have kids fold two layers of tissue paper accordion style. Wedge the tissue paper between the prongs of the doll pin, centering it. Spread the layers to create butterfly wings. Secure the wings with glue on each side.

Have kids decorate the butterfly's wings by dabbing them with glue and applying glitter. Kids can each paint their butterfly's body. Have them make antennae by curling half-lengths of chenille wire around a pencil and attaching them to the butterfly's head with glue.

Use yarn to string the caterpillar and butterfly together once they've dried. Hang the mobiles in your classroom or send them home with kids.

CHRISTMAS CONE

Kids will love making these gift cones for their families for Christmas.

WHAT YOU'LL NEED:

You'll need 8-inch squares of construction paper, 5x10-inch strips of tissue paper, 10-inch pieces of ribbon, stickers, glue, scissors, and individually wrapped candies.

ALLERGY ALERT
See page 10.

FOR EXTRA IMPACT:

- Read aloud **Matthew 2:10-11,** and ask kids how Mary might've felt when the wise men gave baby Jesus gifts.

- Have kids share how it feels to give gifts and how it feels to receive gifts.

- Ask kids: Why do we give gifts? Let kids choose a special person to give their Christmas Cone to and tell the group who they chose and why.

DIRECTIONS

Have each child roll the square into a cone shape, and glue the overlapping edges of the construction paper together. Trim away the excess paper to make the top of the cone level. Glue the tissue paper inside the cone 1 inch from the top, with the remaining tissue sticking above the edge. Decorate the cone with stickers. Fill the cone with candies and tie the tissue with a ribbon.

CHRISTMAS WALL HANGING

Kids create this wall hanging as a Christmas keepsake.

WHAT YOU'LL NEED:

You'll need 20x36-inch white cotton fabric; a 24-inch wooden dowel, 1 inch in diameter; and a 36-inch red ribbon for each wall hanging. You'll also need green, red, and yellow acrylic fabric paint; pinking shears; and a hot glue gun.

FOR EXTRA IMPACT:

- Create a classroom bulletin board by having kids paint their handprints to create a large tree. Let kids decorate the tree and write their names on their handprints.

- Have kids share their favorite Christmas memories.

- Have kids sing their favorite Christmas carols and march around the room carrying their banners.

DIRECTIONS

Before kids arrive, use pinking shears to trim all the edges of the fabric to prevent fraying. Outline a base for a tree at the bottom of the fabric with yellow paint. Using the red paint, write in the child's name and the year.

Have kids each dip their hands one at a time in green paint and place their handprints on their fabric to create the tree. Have kids make four to five handprints across the bottom and work up to the top with only one handprint to form the tree. Decorate the tree by painting a yellow star on top and adding "lights" with the red and yellow paint. Allow to dry.

Place a wooden dowel at the top edge of the hanging. Fold the edge of the fabric down around the dowel to the back of the hanging and glue into place. Tie the ribbon onto both ends of the dowel. Glue the ribbon to the dowel to create a hanger.

CHRISTMAS WREATH

Kids make colorful wreaths to decorate their refrigerators.

WHAT YOU'LL NEED:

You'll need plastic dessert plates, plastic wrap, Elmer's School Glue, magnets, and an old 500- or 1,000-piece jigsaw puzzle. Several days before class, spray paint three-fourths of the puzzle pieces green and the remaining pieces red. Allow these to dry.

FOR EXTRA IMPACT:

- Have kids share ways their families celebrate Christmas.

- Let kids make wreaths to give to neighbors or friends. Have kids color Christmas cards to give along with the wreaths.

- Use extra puzzle pieces and let kids make holly leaves and berries.

DIRECTIONS

Cover a plastic dessert plate with a piece of plastic wrap. Lay several green puzzle pieces around the inner circle of the dessert plate. Overlap the puzzle piece edges, and use Elmer's School Glue to glue the pieces together in the circle. Continue this process with two layers of green pieces on top of the first layer, with all layers glued together. Glue several red pieces here and there on the green pieces to resemble holly berries.

Allow the pieces to dry thoroughly. Then carefully peel the wreath from the plastic wrap. Trim away any excess plastic wrap. Attach a magnet to the back of the wreath so kids can hang their creations on their refrigerators.

CINNAMON ORNAMENTS

Kids make these ornaments to express love to their mothers.

WHAT YOU'LL NEED:

You'll need a Bible, 1 cup ground cinnamon, 1 ½ to 2 cups flour, 2 cups water, rolling pins, pencils, and fishing line.

FOR EXTRA IMPACT:

- Have kids sit in a circle and toss a beanbag or ball back and forth. As kids catch the ball, they should shout ways they can honor their mothers.

- Challenge kids to pick their favorite way and honor their mother with that action during the week.

- Let kids decorate lunch sacks with markers, stickers, and ribbons. Kids can use these to wrap their ornaments after they've dried.

▶ DIRECTIONS

Before kids arrive, boil the water in a medium saucepan. Remove from heat, and stir in the cinnamon. Add the flour ½ cup at a time and stir well. Knead the last half of the flour into the dough after it has cooled slightly. Keep the dough in a container with a tight lid.

Have kids lightly flour a work area and roll out a piece of dough. They should mold it into a shape that reminds them of their mother, such as a heart, a smile, or a helping hand. Use a pencil to make a hole at the top of the shape. String fishing line through the hole and tie a knot to make a hanger. Tell kids to take their ornaments home and let them dry for one to two days, then give to their mother, grandmother, or another special person so she can enjoy its fragrance.

Read aloud **Ephesians 6:2.** Ask: What does it mean to honor your mother? Why does God want us to honor our mothers? How can you honor your mother?

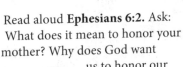

CONTAINER CREATURES

Kids learn that God looks at the heart.

WHAT YOU'LL NEED:

You'll need an opaque container with candy or treats inside, empty oatmeal or cornmeal containers, construction paper, markers, 12-inch pieces of rope or yarn, large wooden beads or empty thread spools, pompoms, glue or tape, and scissors.

FOR EXTRA IMPACT:

- Read aloud **1 Samuel 16:7**, and ask kids: Why do we often judge people by the way they look on the outside? Why does God look at our hearts?

- Let kids fill their Container Creatures with candy treats to remind them that God sees what's on the inside.

ALLERGY ALERT
See page 10.

DIRECTIONS

Have kids each bring a cylinder-shaped cardboard container, such as an oatmeal or cornmeal container, to class.

Hold up the container with treats inside. Say: Would you rather have this container or what's inside it? Explain.

Show the class what's inside the container. Say: Containers are important, but they're not as important as what they hold inside. How is that like or unlike us? How can we learn to see a person's heart and not just the outside?

Give each child a cardboard container. Have children wrap their containers with construction paper. Have them make a fun face with markers, construction paper, and pompoms for noses.

To make the legs, help each child punch two small holes about ¾ inch from the bottom edge and about 2 ½ inches apart under the face. Thread a 12-inch piece of rope or twine in one hole and out the other, pull it through until equal amounts of rope hang out of each hole. Tape the rope on the inside of the container to secure it. Tie a large wooden bead or wooden spool at each end of the rope for feet.

COTTON-BALL VALENTINES

Kids will love this cooperative activity to make fun valentines.

WHAT YOU'LL NEED:

You'll need cotton balls, red construction paper, pens, stamps, envelopes, scissors, glue, and spray perfume. Have extra collage materials on hand, such as wiggly eyes, pompoms, yarn, and chenille stems.

FOR EXTRA IMPACT:

- Have older kids write short verses of Scripture inside the cards.
- Have kids share ways God shows his love for us.
- Let kids choose a special group to send their cards to, such as nursing-home residents.

DIRECTIONS

Have kids work together to form an assembly line. Let younger children do the cutting and gluing while older children draw and write. Work together to produce these cotton-ball valentine cards:

"We love ewe!"—Use cotton balls for a lamb's body. Have kids draw the head and feet. Add wiggly eyes for a fun touch.

"You're sweet!"—Spray a cotton-ball "flower" with perfume, and glue it onto a chenille stem. Draw or cut out tissue-paper petals to add to the flower.

"Our love for you will never end!"—Use a cotton ball for a rabbit's tail. Kids can add a miniature pompom for the bunny nose and make yarn whiskers.

"We love you beary much!"—Use cotton balls for a bear's tummy and head. Use miniature pompoms, or have kids draw the ears and paws. Glue on wiggly eyes.

Have kids think up more ideas. When finished, have older kids address and stamp the envelopes. Younger children can help you mail the cards. And everyone can hand deliver valentines for loved ones nearby.

DANDY LIONS

Kids create a tangible reminder that God's love helps them overcome their fears.

WHAT YOU'LL NEED:

You'll need paper plates, yarn, yellow and brown construction paper, glue, scissors, black face paint and brush, and a hole punch.

FOR EXTRA IMPACT:

- Let kids wear their masks and act out the story of Daniel in the lions' den. Have kids take turns playing Daniel.

- Teach kids this rhyme to say as they leave the lions' den.

  The lions did not hurt me;
  I was lifted from the den.

  I can trust in God
  Again and again.

- For a yummy lion snack, have kids frost cupcakes with yellow icing. Add orange gumdrops cut in half around the edge of the cupcake for the mane, use brown M&M'S candies for eyes, and red shoestring licorice for whiskers.

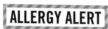

See page 10.

DIRECTIONS

Have kids cut out the center of a white paper plate. Cut several 1x4-inch strips of yellow construction paper. Apply the strips with glue, covering the perimeter of the plate to create a lion's mane. Cut out two brown ears, and glue them on top of the yellow mane. Punch a hole on each side of the plate, and tie a 10-inch piece of yarn through each hole.

Have kids line up to get a black nose and whisker dots once they've got their masks on.

Read aloud **Daniel 6:16-23**. Then ask: How do you think Daniel felt when he was trapped in the lions' den? What would you have done? Why did God keep the lions from hurting Daniel? When you're afraid, how can you trust God the way Daniel did?

DAVID AND SAUL

Kids learn how Jesus wants us to treat our enemies.

WHAT YOU'LL NEED:

You'll need a Bible, newsprint, markers, scissors, construction paper, glue, and tape. Before class, cut a "robe" from newsprint or a brown paper bag.

FOR EXTRA IMPACT:

- Have older kids trace and cut out several handprints and then write on each one a different way they can be kind to others.

- Have kids find a partner and share their helping handprint ideas with one another.

- Borrow some old choir robes, and let kids act out the story of David and Saul.

DIRECTIONS

Have children use markers or crayons to decorate the robe. Then tape it to the wall with the hem at floor level.

Paraphrase the story from **1 Samuel 24**. Then have each child sneak up as quietly as David did and cut off a small piece from the bottom of the robe. Trace around each child's hand on construction paper. Then have children glue their robe remnant to their outlined hand.

Write a paraphrase of **1 Samuel 24:11** on each child's sheet of construction paper. For example, write, "A piece of your robe is in my hand, but I did not harm you."

Ask children: Has anyone ever made you angry? Tell us about it. Did you ever want to hurt someone who hurt you?

Say: King Saul wanted to hurt David. King Saul was an enemy to David, but David treated King Saul kindly. Listen to what Jesus says he wants us to do to our enemies.

From an easy-to-understand translation, read aloud **Luke 6:27-31**.

Ask: Why does God want us to be kind to all people? How can we be kind to people who are mean to us?

Close in prayer, asking God to help kids be kind to people even when they are mean.

EASTER EGG PIÑATA

Kids love making this festive craft to celebrate Easter.

WHAT YOU'LL NEED:

You'll need an inflated and tied-off balloon, dozens of newspaper strips (approximately 2x8-inches), and a 2x10-inch cardboard strip for each child. You'll also need a craft knife, paint, paintbrushes, individually wrapped candies, string, duct tape, stapler, a thin mixture of plaster of Paris in a pie plate or other open container, towels for cleanup, a hair dryer, and paint smocks or old T-shirts for children to wear.

FOR EXTRA IMPACT:

- Have kids share ways their families celebrate Easter.

- Read aloud **Luke 24:45-47**, and have kids discuss the real meaning of Easter.

DIRECTIONS

Before class, cover your work area with newspapers. Have kids each staple a cardboard strip into a "crown" and place it under their balloon to help it stand up. Dip a newspaper strip into the plaster of Paris mixture and then remove the excess mixture by running the strip between their index and middle fingers. Have kids lay their lightly coated strip on their balloon and smooth it down so it lays flat on the balloon. Repeat this process until the entire balloon is covered by two layers of strips. Help kids achieve uniformity in covering their balloons for best results.

Allow the balloons to dry for one week. Have kids cut two small holes in the top of their balloons and remove the fragments. Have kids paint the outside of their balloon shells, and allow the paint to dry. Use a hair dryer to speed the drying time.

Have kids put candy into their piñatas, tie a string through the opening in the top, and duct tape around the opening. Let kids take their piñatas home and enjoy batting them until they break.

ALLERGY ALERT
See page 10.

EDIBLE MANGER SCENES

Kids will have a multi-sensory experience of Christ's nativity.

WHAT YOU'LL NEED:

You'll need a Bible, graham crackers, animal crackers, elf-shape cookies, shredded-wheat biscuits, chocolate stars, miniature pretzels, marshmallows, one 8x10-inch piece of cardboard for each child, foil, blunt knives, and "frosting glue." Make frosting glue by mixing ½ pound powdered sugar, 2 egg whites, and ¼ teaspoon cream of tartar. Beat 7 to 10 minutes. Refrigerate in a tightly covered container.

FOR EXTRA IMPACT:

- Have kids get in pairs and take turns retelling the Christmas story using their manger scenes.

- To make a quick stable, cut a door in a pint-size milk carton. Have kids cover the carton with canned chocolate frosting and press crumbled shredded wheat onto the frosting.

- Let kids draw a manger scene tracing around cookie cutters to make animals and people.

ALLERGY ALERT
See page 10.

DIRECTIONS

Have kids wrap a cardboard piece in foil to use as a base. Use the frosting glue to form a graham-cracker stable on the base. Dip the edges of crackers into the frosting glue, and hold the edges of two crackers together for one minute while the frosting sets. Have kids build three walls before adding the roof.

Add people and animals to the scene. Crumble shredded-wheat biscuits to add hay. Use frosting to attach a marshmallow to the center of a pretzel to make an angel. Glue the angel and a chocolate star to the top of the stable.

Read aloud **Luke 2:1-20**. Ask: Why do you think God allowed Jesus to be born in a stable? If you could've chosen a place for Jesus to be born, where would you have chosen? Explain. What difference has Jesus' birth and life made for you?

FIRECRACKERS

Kids learn to shine bright for Jesus.

WHAT YOU'LL NEED:

You'll need a Bible; toilet-paper tubes; various colors of long, metallic-paper strips; star stickers; glitter; glue; construction paper; and scissors.

FOR EXTRA IMPACT:

- Have kids tell good deeds they'll do during the week to honor God.

- Tape colorful metallic-paper strips to the end of a flashlight. Turn off the lights, and let the kids shine the flashlight to create shimmering firework effects.

- Kids can make colorful bookmarks by stapling metallic strips to the end of a piece of cardstock. Then write on the cardstock, "Let your light shine!"

DIRECTIONS

Have kids each decorate a toilet-paper tube with stickers, glitter, and construction paper. Cut out a circle of construction paper big enough to cover the bottom of the tube. Glue the circle to the tube, and glue long strips of metallic paper inside the tube so they dangle out the open end.

Read aloud **Matthew 5:16**. How is God's love like or unlike a firecracker? Once you've experienced God's love, what do you want to do with it? What are things we can do to shine bright like fireworks with Jesus' love?

FLAME BOUQUETS

Kids make "flame" bouquets for Pentecost Sunday.

WHAT YOU'LL NEED:

You'll need flame-colored cellophane or tissue paper, gold foil, scissors, florists' wire, crepe-paper streamers, construction paper, and markers.

FOR EXTRA IMPACT:

- Throw a party to celebrate that Pentecost is the birthday of the church. Have cake, balloons, games, and all the trimmings.

- Read aloud **Acts 2:1-4,** and have kids share ways the Holy Spirit helps us.

- Cut strawberries vertically to create wedge-shape slices. Have kids fill ice-cream cones with frozen yogurt and then press the strawberry "flames" into the top of the yogurt for a "fiery" treat.

ALLERGY ALERT

See page 10.

DIRECTIONS

Cut flame-colored cellophane or tissue and gold foil into 4x8-inch rectangles. Layer seven pieces on top of each other. Then fan out the pieces so all the colors show. Gather the rectangles 2 inches from the bottom. Wrap florists' wire and two 2-foot crepe-paper streamers around the gathered end.

Have kids use construction paper and markers to make appreciation cards. Make one card to go along with each bouquet. Kids can present them to church helpers, such as the pastor, teachers, and volunteers.

FLOWERPOT SCULPTURES

Kids can create beautiful, hand-picked flower gifts this Mother's Day.

WHAT YOU'LL NEED:

You'll need small foam cups, potting soil, assorted potting flowers, and 12-inch pieces of aluminum foil.

FOR EXTRA IMPACT:

- Let older kids paint small clay pots with nontoxic shiny paints to use for the planters.

- Using a lightweight blanket, have kids stand in a circle and each grab hold of an edge of the blanket. Have kids raise their hands, lifting the blanket overhead, and yell out ways God's love covers us.

- Read aloud **Psalm 52:8,** and have kids share ways we can trust in God's unfailing love.

DIRECTIONS

Have kids think of the person they want to give a gift to and then choose a flower that reminds them of that person. Kids might choose a beautiful flower because Mom is beautiful or a tall flower because Aunt Jean is tall. Ask kids to tell why they chose their flowers.

Have kids transplant their flowers into foam cups, adding potting soil as needed. Have them place their cup in the center of a piece of foil and press the foil around the cup's base and sides.

Say: God loves the person you're thinking of very much. His love covers us, like the foil covers the cup.

Have kids creatively sculpt the foil to create a shimmering, delightful flowerpot that represents God's love for the flower recipient. Close in prayer, thanking God for the children and his love for everyone.

FOOTPRINTS IN THE SAND

Kids make imprints of their feet to remind them to walk with God.

WHAT YOU'LL NEED:

You'll need large sheets of black plastic, sand, plaster of Paris, water, a mixing bucket, and metal eyelets.

FOR EXTRA IMPACT:

- Read aloud a copy of the poem "Footprints in the Sand" by Mary Stevenson. You can find a copy of the poem online or at your local library.

- Ask kids: How can we follow God and serve him?

- Ask kids: How does it feel to know God carries us during hard times? Close in prayer, thanking God for being with us always.

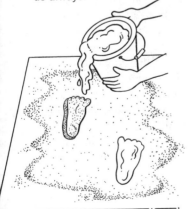

DIRECTIONS

Lay out sheets of black plastic. Pour 3 inches of sand onto sections of the black plastic, one for each child. Mix enough water into the sand so it'll hold a mold. Mix the plaster of Paris and water in the bucket according to the directions.

Have each child press one foot 2 inches into a sand section. Carefully pour plaster into each footprint. Then insert one metal eyelet in each print to hang it later. Clean out the eyelet opening if necessary. The plaster takes 30 minutes to harden.

While prints are drying, read aloud from **Joshua 22:5**: "Love the Lord your God, to walk in all his ways, to obey his commands, to hold fast to him, and to serve him with all your heart and all your soul." Ask: What does it means to walk in God's ways?

Once the plaster has hardened, gently dig out the footprints and brush off the excess sand. The footprints should dry overnight before being hung on the wall.

GARDEN-IN-A-POT

Kids celebrate God's gifts of nature with these colorful gardens.

WHAT YOU'LL NEED:

You'll need 4-inch clay pots; green floral foam; 4-inch plastic-foam balls cut in half; black chenille wires; cotton swabs; wiggle eyes; extra-wide, extra-long, jumbo craft sticks; ³⁄₁₆-inch wooden dowels in 12-inch lengths; red, black, and yellow nontoxic acrylic paint; and a hot glue gun.

FOR EXTRA IMPACT:

- Have kid make butterflies by coloring coffee filters with markers and crayons. Pinch the filter in the middle, add a chenille wire folded in half for the antennae, and clip together with a clothes-pin.

- Let kids fill in their gardens with artificial or tissue-paper flowers.

DIRECTIONS

Have kids make the following items for their gardens:

Pots—Have each child paint a 4-inch clay pot. When the paint is dry, fill the pot with floral foam. Help children use a hot glue gun to tack the sides of the foam to the pot.

Ladybugs—Give each child half of a plastic-foam ball. Have each child cover the foam-ball half with red paint. When the paint is dry, paint black dots using a cotton swab. Glue on two movable craft eyes. Push black chenille wires into the plastic foam for the legs and antennae. Push a wooden dowel into the flat side of the ladybug, and insert the dowel into the foam in the pot.

Sunflowers—Have each child cover half of a plastic-foam ball with black paint. While the paint dries, each child can paint 10 craft sticks bright yellow. When the paint is dry, push the craft sticks around the outer edge of the foam ball to create the petals of the sunflower. Push a wooden dowel into the base of the rounded side of the sunflower (behind the petals), and insert the stick into the foam in the pot.

GETHSEMANE SNACKS

Kids make this tasty snack as a reminder of Jesus' time in Gethsemane.

WHAT YOU'LL NEED:

You'll need a Bible, graham crackers, gummy worms, chocolate-covered raisins, pretzel sticks, small marshmallows, resealable baggies, paper plates, napkins, and plastic spoons.

ALLERGY ALERT
See page 10.

FOR EXTRA IMPACT:

- As kids eat their snacks, ask: Why did the disciples flee? How do you think Jesus felt when everyone left him?

- Read aloud **Mark 14:49,** and explain to kids what it means that the "Scriptures must be fulfilled."

- Tell kids that **Isaiah 53** was written long before Jesus was ever born and foretells Jesus' death for our sins.

DIRECTIONS

Read aloud **Mark 14:32-50**. As you narrate the biblical account, have kids or volunteers distribute paper plates and then pass out the snack ingredients that go with the story.

Give kids crumbled graham crackers and chocolate-covered raisins to represent the ground and rocks where Jesus knelt. Children should pour the "sand" onto the paper plate and scatter "rocks."

Gummy worms represent the disciples' temptation to fall asleep. Marshmallows represent the soft places where the disciples rested their heads and slept. Pretzel sticks represent the swords and clubs carried by the men who came to arrest Jesus.

GIFT FOR MOM

Kids express their love to their mom or another special woman.

WHAT YOU'LL NEED:

You'll need a clear 35-mm film canister for each child (available from photo processors), 1-inch-wide ribbon or fabric strips, narrow ribbon or rickrack, fabric paints, yarn, sequins or beads, tacky glue, scissors, paintbrush, egg carton, poster board, and small candies.

FOR EXTRA IMPACT:

- Read aloud **1 Corinthians 13:4,** and have kids share ways their moms show them love.

- Have kids tell ways they can show love to their moms. Encourage kids to do at least one of those things during the week.

- Let kids each make an affirmation gift bag by writing words that describe their mom on the outside of a paper lunch sack, placing the gift inside, and tying with colorful ribbon.

▶ DIRECTIONS

Have kids work with the open end of the canister up. Glue the wide ribbon or fabric strip around the bottom half of the film canister. Then glue narrow ribbon or rickrack along the top edge of the wide ribbon.

Remove the canister's cap and set it aside. Paint a face on the canister with fabric paint. Cut and unravel yarn pieces and glue them around the back and sides of the canister for hair. Add sequins or beads for earrings.

Cut and paint an egg carton section to make a hat. When the paint is dry, bend up a brim around the edge. Add ribbons or sequins for decoration.

Cut a 3-inch-diameter circle from poster board. Print ,"God fills Moms with LOVE!" around the outside edge of the circle. Glue the film canister to the middle of the circle. Fill the canister with small candies, replace the cap, and put the hat on it. Then give it to Mom!

GOD'S BLOSSOMS

Kids learn to trust God to take care of all their needs.

WHAT YOU'LL NEED:

You'll need a Bible, eggshell halves, acrylic paints, paintbrushes, green chenille wires, and a hot-glue gun.

FOR EXTRA IMPACT:

- Let kids cut out and tape tissue paper leaves onto their flower stems.
- Use the inside of the eggs to make scrambled eggs for a snack.
- As kids eat the scrambled eggs, have them share ways God takes care of us.

▶ DIRECTIONS

Before kids arrive, carefully crack the eggs you use so you have two intact eggshell halves. Wash the shells, and let them dry. Poke a small hole in the bottom of each shell.

Give kids each an eggshell half to paint any color they want with acrylic paint. Allow the shells to dry. Then insert a green chenille stem through the hole, and hot-glue the tip inside the egg.

Read aloud **Matthew 6:25-34**. Discuss with kids that we don't need to worry about our lives because God is always taking care of us. Tell kids that whenever they see flowers, they can remember that God is taking care of them, even as he takes care of the "little" things.

ALLERGY ALERT

See page 10.

GRASS SEED SAMSON

Kids love making a version of the Chia Pet planter...only it's a Chia Samson!

WHAT YOU'LL NEED:

You'll need one rinsed ½-pint milk carton for each child, potting soil, grass seed, construction paper, fine-tipped markers, and glue sticks.

FOR EXTRA IMPACT:

- Tell kids how God gave Samson a special gift of strength, but Delilah stole his strength. Read aloud **Judges 16:15-19.**

- Ask kids: What are some special gifts God has given you?

- Let kids each make a Samson snack by decorating a frosted cookie with dried fruit or candy for the face and shoestring licorice for Samson's hair.

ALLERGY ALERT
See page 10.

DIRECTIONS

Give each child a ½-pint milk carton. Open the top of the milk carton so the carton becomes an open cube. Have kids glue construction paper around the carton to cover the milk logo. Then let kids draw a Samson face (up to the forehead) on the construction paper. The top of the carton is the hairline.

Fill each carton with potting soil to about half an inch from the top. Then sprinkle grass seed on the soil, and cover the seed with a thin layer of soil.

Set the "Samsons" in a sunny windowsill and keep them well watered. After a few days, each Samson's hair will begin to grow! Once it gets a few inches long, kids can cut the "hair."

GUMDROP FLOWERS

Kids love making these edible flowers.

WHAT YOU'LL NEED:

You'll need large gumdrop candies, rolling pins, sugar, wax paper, scissors, and plastic sandwich bags.

ALLERGY ALERT

See page 10.

FOR EXTRA IMPACT:

- Read aloud **1 Peter 1:24-25.** Ask kids what they think the passage means.

- Have kids eat their flower petals one at a time and compare how that is like or unlike what happens when flowers wither and fall away.

- Have kids write, "'The word of the Lord stands forever' 1 Peter 1:25" on card-stock strips. Kids can use the strips as bookmarks in their Bibles to remind them of the strength of God's Word.

DIRECTIONS

Have kids each cut large gumdrops in half and use the halves to design a flower on a sugared piece of wax paper. They can use one sliced gumdrop for the center and halves of different colors for the petals. They can use green gumdrops to form the stems and petals.

After kids design their flowers, they can sprinkle sugar on the candies to keep them from sticking. Have kids roll out the flowers, then carefully slide them into plastic sandwich bags.

HEART MARKS

Kids make these decorative bookmarks as a perfect outreach gift for patients in the hospital or homebound church members.

WHAT YOU'LL NEED:

You'll need 1½x5-inch craft-foam strips and craft-foam scraps of various colors. You'll also need scissors, glue, a hole punch, multicolored yarn, a Bible, and permanent fine-tipped markers.

FOR EXTRA IMPACT:

- Have kids each write, "'Give thanks to the God of gods. His love endures forever'—Psalm 136:2" on the back of their bookmarks.

- Have kids tell ways they've seen God's love in their lives.

- Close in prayer, and encourage each child to give thanks to God for one thing.

▶ DIRECTIONS

Give each child a 1½x5-inch craft-foam strip. Have kids cut 10 hearts of various sizes from the craft-foam scraps. The hearts can be of any color and must be small enough to fit on the foam strip.

Have kids arrange and then glue the hearts to the craft-foam strips. Then have them punch a single hole at the top center of the bookmark.

To finish the bookmarks, have kids each cut six 10-inch lengths of the multicolored yarn. Hold the yarn pieces with the ends even. Fold the yarn pieces in half, and push the fold through the hole at the top center of the bookmark to create a 1-inch loop. Pull the yarn ends through the loop and gently pull to make a snug knot.

HUMAN BEANS

Kids can use this outreach craft as a great way to send a loving message to friends and neighbors.

WHAT YOU'LL NEED:

You'll need a 16-inch section of nylon tights including the foot for each child. You'll also need dried beans, wiggle eyes, glue, craft foam, pompoms, scissors, card stock, curling ribbon, yarn, a hole punch, and glitter pens.

FOR EXTRA IMPACT:

- Read aloud **Psalm 52:8,** and have kids tell ways we can trust in God's unfailing love.

- Ask kids: How is reaching out to others like or unlike a tree flourishing in God's love?

- Have kids write, "'I trust in God's unfailing love for ever and ever'—Psalm 52:8b" on the back of the human bean cards.

DIRECTIONS

Give kids each a section of tights. Have them fill the foot of the tights with dried beans until the section is about two-thirds full, then tie a knot around the open end of the tights. Have kids cut the remainder of the tights in thin strips to make hair or fold the remainder over the top of the knot for a hat.

Have kids cut out two feet from craft foam and then glue them to the bottom of the "human bean." Allow the glue to dry. Have kids decorate their human beans with wiggle eyes and pompom noses.

Have kids fold a 3x5-inch piece of card stock in half and cut out a bean-shaped card. Have them write, "From one human bean to another— God loves you!" on the cards. Punch a hole in the cards, and use curling ribbon to attach them to the beans. Kids can give their human beans to friends and family.

FROM ONE HUMAN BEAN TO ANOTHER— GOD LOVES YOU!

LEAFY T'S

Kids learn about God's creation.

WHAT YOU'LL NEED:

You'll need a Bible, newspaper, fabric paints, paintbrushes, container of water, prewashed solid T-shirt for each child, small craft sponges, and fresh, green leaves. You'll need to press the green leaves between layers of newspaper for one week prior to use.

FOR EXTRA IMPACT:

- Take kids on a nature hike to collect leaves, pine cones, and other natural items for a classroom display. While hiking, talk about God's creation.

- Make a classroom banner by letting kids stamp the leaves onto muslin or cotton fabric. Use a paint pen to write the words to **Revelation 4:11** on the banner. Attach ribbon to the top as a hanger.

- Make earth-friendly greeting cards by stamping paint-coated leaves onto recycled paper.

DIRECTIONS

Cover the work area with newspaper. Fold newspaper inside the body and sleeves of the T-shirts. Then lay the shirt on the table, and smooth out any wrinkles.

Have kids wet a paintbrush and squeeze most of the water out of it. Use the brush to coat a sponge with one color of paint. Carefully dab the sponge on the veined side of the leaf, including the stem. Have kids turn the leaf over and use their fingers to gently press it onto the T-shirt. Tell kids to press, but not to rub the leaves. Pick the leaf up by the stem and check the print. Add more or less paint next time as needed. Leave the newspaper inside the shirt until it's dry.

Read aloud **Revelation 4:11**. What does this verse teach us about how we should respond to God when we look at creation?

LET IT SHINE

Kids learn to light the path to faith in Christ on Halloween.

WHAT YOU'LL NEED:

You'll need lunch sacks, cookie cutters, pencils, votive candles, and sand.

FOR EXTRA IMPACT:

- Read aloud **Psalm 119:105**. Have kids share ways God's Word lights their path.

- Read aloud **Matthew 5:14-16**. Challenge kids to think of a good deed that can be a light to others during the week.

- Have kids share ways we can be God's light for the world at Halloween.

DIRECTIONS

Explain to kids that a luminaria is used to light a path. Distribute lunch sacks, and have kids trace cookie cutters to make hearts, crosses, or other shapes on the sacks. Then have them use pencils to poke holes through the sacks about ¼ inch apart around the traced shapes. Have kids pour enough sand in the sacks to cover the bottoms. Give each child a votive candle to place in the sack and light at home. Be sure kids know that parents need to light their candles and supervise the use of the luminarias.

Close in prayer, asking God to help people who live in darkness see the light of Christ and trust him as their Savior.

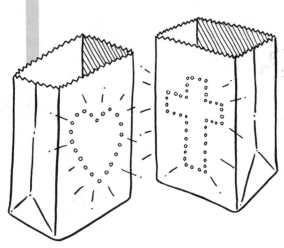

LITTLE LAMB CARDS

Kids make little lambs to celebrate the Lamb of God.

WHAT YOU'LL NEED:

You'll need a half sheet of 8½ x11-inch card stock folded in half, a small jingle bell, and a white chenille wire for each lamb. You'll also need red-ink stamp pads, black markers, pencils, cotton balls, glue, and scissors.

FOR EXTRA IMPACT:

- Read aloud **John 1:29**. Have older kids write the words to the verse inside their cards.

- Ask kids: What does it mean that Jesus takes away the sin of the world?

- Close in prayer thanking God for sending Jesus, the Lamb of God, to die for our sins.

DIRECTIONS

Have kids press a fingertip onto the stamp pad and then to the left of the card front's center. The fingerprint is the lamb's head. Pencil in an oval to outline the lamb's body. Have kids glue cotton balls inside the outline and then draw ears, eyes, nose, and feet with a marker.

Attach a bell by inserting a chenille wire through the bell's loop and punching the wire ends through the card stock at the lamb's neck. Twist the wire ends to secure the bell, and trim away the excess wire. Have kids write their names inside their cards.

MACARONI NAME TAGS

Kids learn about the meaning of names.

WHAT YOU'LL NEED:

For the name tags, you'll need glue, toothpicks, uncooked alphabet macaroni, markers, and bar pins. You'll also need a names book and a Bible.

FOR EXTRA IMPACT:

- Use a blow dryer to speed drying time of the name tags. Let older kids dry their own name tags.

- Let kids write their name and its meaning on construction paper. Have markers, ribbons, and other collage materials on hand to decorate.

- Have kids draw a separate picture of each family member and write the person's name and its meanings on the paper. Draw a title page, and write, "My Family Names Book," on it. Then put the pictures together and staple them to form a book.

DIRECTIONS

Have kids glue five toothpicks together, side by side. While the glue dries, let kids use the alphabet macaroni to spell their names and then use different color markers to decorate the macaroni.

Have kids glue their name to the toothpicks and then glue the back of a bar pin to the back of the toothpicks. Let dry.

Read aloud **Matthew 16:17-18**. Say: Jesus changed Simon's name to *Peter*, which means "rock." How many of you know what your name means?

Use a names book to find the meaning of children's names. Say: Just as Jesus helped Peter be a strong rock for the church, God also helps the meaning of your name be true.

FRONT

BACK

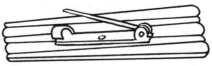

MEMORABLE MONTAGE

Kids create place mats to celebrate thankfulness.

WHAT YOU'LL NEED:

You'll need one 12x18-inch sheet of construction paper, photos, scissors, glue, and clear Con-Tact paper. Have kids bring in copies of their favorite old photos.

FOR EXTRA IMPACT:

- Have kids turn to a partner to share a Thanksgiving memory.

- Let kids make place mats for family members to use as memorable Thanksgiving-meal table decorations and a discussion starter about thankfulness.

- Read aloud **Acts 27:35,** and ask kids to tell why it's important for us to give thanks to God.

DIRECTIONS

Have kids cut and arrange their photos to make a collage on one side of their construction paper. If kids don't have photos, give them magazines, and let them cut out pictures of things they're thankful for.

Glue the photos and pictures to the paper and allow to dry. To protect the place mat, carefully cover both sides with Con-Tact paper.

Have kids each choose one photo or picture from their place mat and share why they're thankful for what it shows. Close with a prayer thanking God for all the wonderful things he gives us.

MINI EASTER GARDEN

Kids learn about the garden tomb that was empty Easter morning.

WHAT YOU'LL NEED:

You'll need garden soil; moss, cut grass, or sand; craft sticks; glue; small pots; flat stones large enough to cover the pots; egg-carton cups (or other small containers); small flowers; and gravel. You'll also need a shallow dish or tray for each child.

FOR EXTRA IMPACT:

- Read aloud **Luke 24:5-8,** and ask kids why they think the women were afraid. Ask: How do you think you would have felt?

- Ask: How do you think the women felt when they realized Jesus had risen from the dead? How does that make you feel today?

- Give each child a hollow chocolate Easter egg as a reminder to celebrate the empty tomb.

ALLERGY ALERT

See page 10.

DIRECTIONS

Have kids each fill a tray with soil and arrange the soil to make a hill on one side of the tray and a flat area on the other. Cover the soil with moss, grass, or sand.

Make crosses with the craft sticks and glue. Then place them on the hilltop. Press the small pot into the "hillside" to make a cave or tomb. Place the stone over the mouth of the tomb.

Press the egg cups into the soil around the flat "garden" area and fill them with the small flowers. Use gravel to make a path to the tomb to show how the disciples ran there on Easter morning.

When the scenes are completed, gather children around the gardens and retell the Easter story. As you tell about the rock being rolled away, have children move the stones from their "tombs" to show that they're empty.

MUSICAL INSTRUMENTS

Kids create a joyful noise with these exciting musical instruments.

WHAT YOU'LL NEED:

You'll need paper plates, soft-drink bottle tops, heavy thread, large beads, wooden dowels, metal jar lids, staplers, masking tape, ice pick (for adult use only), ¼-inch elastic, glue, hole punch, and scissors.

FOR EXTRA IMPACT:

- Read aloud **Psalm 98:4-6,** and ask kids: How does God feel when we praise him? How does it feel to praise God with our music? Explain.

- Let kids form a praise band. Put on praise music, and let kids play along with their instruments.

- Let kids perform their praise music for other classes.

DIRECTIONS

Twirling drums—Have kids staple two facing paper plates together around the edges. Punch two holes along the edges on opposite sides of the plates. Tie a large bead to an 8-inch section of heavy duty thread, and tie the other end through one hole on each plate. Repeat this for the second hole. Tape a wooden dowel on the center edge of the plates below the two holes. Once the dowel is attached, kids will roll the dowel between their hands to twirl the drum and create a unique beat.

Tambourines—Have kids staple two facing paper plates together around the edges. Use a hole punch to make eight evenly spaced holes around the edges of the plates. Have an adult use an ice pick to punch a hole in the center of bottle tops. Kids can string two bottle tops on 3-inch pieces of heavy-duty thread and then tie the thread through the holes in the edges of the plates. Keep the bottle tops on the same side of the plate.

Castanets—Have an adult use an ice pick to punch two holes in metal jar lids. Each child will need four lids to make a set of castanets. Have kids tie 3-inch sections of ¼-inch elastic through the holes and cut off any extra. Kids will wear one castanet on each thumb and the other on their forefingers or middle fingers.

PRAYER GARDENS

Kids learn how prayer causes wonderful things to grow.

WHAT YOU'LL NEED:

You'll need an egg carton for each child, markers, stickers, rubber bands, potting soil, and flower seeds.

FOR EXTRA IMPACT:

- Read aloud **Psalm 17:6,** and have kids share different ways we can call on God to hear our prayers.

- Have kids share praise reports of ways God has answered their prayers.

- Have older kids write out Psalm 17:6. Encourage kids to read the Scripture each day before saying their prayer-garden prayers.

DIRECTIONS

Give each child an egg carton. Have children use markers and stickers to create a garden scene inside the carton top. Then fill each egg cup with soil and a flower seed. Secure the lids with rubber bands so children can safely transport their cartons.

Ask kids to think of someone with a problem. Encourage them to pray daily for that person and then add ⅛ teaspoon of water to each egg cup. Say: When we pray for people, God causes wonderful things to grow in their lives.

Send a note home with children, telling parents to transplant the seedlings soon after sprouts appear.

PRAYER WHEEL

Kids create a fun way to bring the habit of prayer to their family table.

WHAT YOU'LL NEED:

You'll need a Bible, poster board, marker, scissors, brads, glue, paintbrushes, paint, pens, paint shirts, a table cover, and a hair dryer.

FOR EXTRA IMPACT:

- Have kids share ways they've seen God answer prayers.

- Help kids reinforce the habit of mealtime prayers by having them say a blessing before each snack.

- Make a prayer wheel for the class with each child's name in one of the pie sections. Let kids use the wheel to kick off prayer time before each class begins.

DIRECTIONS

Have kids tell about their mealtime prayers at home. Ask kids to choose three favorite things their family or someone else's family prays for. Number the things 1, 2, and 3, and list them on the edge of a 5x5-inch square of poster board. Draw a pie chart on the poster board, and divide the chart to make a section for each family member. Write a family member's name in each piece.

Make a poster-board spinner by pushing a brad through the end of a poster board arrow and into the center of the pie chart. Have kids decorate their prayer wheels. Let kids use the hair dryer to dry any paint.

Read aloud **Acts 27:35.** Ask: Why does God want us to pray to him? How often does your family pray together?

Say: Use this prayer wheel at mealtimes to help your family remember to pray. Spin the arrow, and the person whose name it lands on says the prayer that night. If that person can't think of anything to pray for, have him or her choose one of the numbered items on the wheel.

PULLED PALMS

Kids make palm branches to celebrate Jesus.

WHAT YOU'LL NEED:

You'll need scissors, glue, and 8 sheets of paper for each palm branch.

FOR EXTRA IMPACT:

- Read aloud **Mark 11:1-10,** and have kids share how they think Jesus would arrive into town today.

- Choose a child to play Jesus, and have him or her parade around your room while the other kids wave their palm branches.

- Lead kids in singing their favorite praise song as they wave their palms to the music.

DIRECTIONS

To make a palm branch, roll the first paper lengthwise into a ½-inch tube. When halfway rolled, lay another sheet of paper on top of the unrolled portion. Continue rolling until the second sheet is rolled halfway. Add additional pieces of paper in the same manner. Glue the last edge in place.

Then cut slits approximately 2-inches long and ¼-inch wide around one end of the tube. Gently pull the paper from the center of the roll. Twist the roll slightly as you pull. Brush the paper fringes to make them stand out.

Now you're ready for a Palm Sunday procession. Have children wave their palms as you lead them in this rhyming cheer:

Who do we want? Jesus!

Why do we want him? He's our King!

How do we praise him? With our palms!

When do we praise him? When we sing!

RAINBOW LIGHT CATCHER

Kids learn to cooperate with this colorful craft.

WHAT YOU'LL NEED:

You'll need a Bible; clear Con-tact paper; scissors; pencil or crayon; masking tape; several sheets of red, orange, yellow, green, and blue tissue paper; cotton balls; hole punch; and string.

FOR EXTRA IMPACT:

- Have kids share some of the promises we have from God.

- Let kids talk about the people who are most trustworthy in their lives and why they can be trusted.

- Let kids make a miniature version of the rainbow to take home and hang in their rooms as a reminder of their promise to cooperate with others.

DIRECTIONS

Before kids arrive, unwind a 5-foot section of Con-tact paper, with the backing still on it, on a long table. Lay the Con-tact paper lengthwise with the clear side up. Draw the five divisions of a rainbow across it. Turn the paper over and remove the backing so the sticky side is up. Use masking tape at each end to hold it down.

Have kids cut tissue paper into 2-inch squares and place the squares in same-color piles. Pinch the center of each square so the sides of the tissue paper "fan out." Stick the pinched part of each tissue-paper square to the Con-tact paper. Fill each section of the rainbow with many pieces of tissue paper. The colors in a rainbow are in this order: red, orange, yellow, green, and blue.

Fill in the remaining areas of the Con-tact paper with cotton balls to make clouds. Using the hole punch, make holes 4 inches from the top, and string up the rainbow in an open area so light can show through it.

Read aloud **Genesis 9:12-17**. Explain that a covenant is an agreement between two people. Say: God made a promise to us. Let's promise to work harder at cooperating with one another.

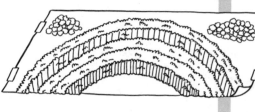

RIBBON PRAYER

This craft is designed to help children learn the Lord's Prayer.

WHAT YOU'LL NEED:

You'll need 4 inches each of blue, white, purple, green, yellow, red, black, and gold ribbon for each child. You'll also need a Bible.

FOR EXTRA IMPACT:

- Have kids choose a favorite song. Let them dance along to the music, waving their prayer ribbons.

- Cut 12-inch construction paper strips for each different ribbon color. Have kids tape the strips to the end of a paper towel tube to make prayer tubes.

- Have kids make extra prayer ribbons to give to friends or family members to teach others about the Lord's Prayer.

DIRECTIONS

Read aloud **Matthew 6:9-13.**

Say: Blue can be a color for fathers. Say, "Our Father in heaven" as you hold the blue ribbon.

White represents holiness. Say, "Hallowed be your name" as you tie the white ribbon to the blue one.

Purple is a majestic color. Say, "Your kingdom come, your will be done" as you tie purple to white.

Green is one of the colors of the earth. Say, "On earth as it is in heaven" as you tie green to purple.

Yellow reminds us of wheat. Say, "Give us today our daily bread" as you tie yellow to green.

Red reminds us of Jesus' blood. By trusting in Jesus, we're forgiven. Say, "And forgive us our debts, as we also have forgiven our debtors" as you tie red to yellow.

Black can represent evil. Say, "And do not lead us into temptation, but deliver us from evil" as you tie black to red.

And gold reminds us of God's heavenly kingdom. Say: "For Thine is the kingdom, and the power, and the glory, forever. Amen." as you tie gold to black.

SAILBOATS

Kids learn to trust God in the storms of life.

WHAT YOU'LL NEED:

For each sailboat, you'll need glue, half of a plastic-foam sandwich box, a 5½x11-inch plastic-foam meat tray, an empty thread spool, and a thin straw. You'll also need a Bible, sails and flags cut from card stock, and a small wading pool filled with water.

FOR EXTRA IMPACT:

- Share with kids about a time in your life that God was trustworthy during a storm.

- Have kids form groups, and give each group a large cardboard box to color to resemble a boat. Then let kids act out Paul's voyage.

- Make sailboat snacks. Press carrot sticks into peeled hard-boiled egg halves. Cut slices of American cheese on the diagonal, and carefully press the triangles around toothpicks to make the sails.

ALLERGY ALERT
See page 10.

▶ DIRECTIONS

Have kids each glue the half of a sandwich box upside down on the upper side of the meat tray to make the ship and its cabin. Next, glue the spool to the top of the sandwich box. Put the straw through the hole in the spool and punch it into the top of the sandwich box (but not through the meat tray). Glue sails and flags to the straw "mast."

Let kids test the seaworthiness of their boats in the wading pool. Then tell them the story of Paul's voyage in **Acts 27.** Ask: How do you think Paul and the sailors felt during the storm? How did God take care of the people on the ship? What are some "storms" or hard things that threaten to shipwreck our lives? How can we trust God to take care of us during those storms?

SAND CASTLE CLAY

Kids learn about God's hidden treasures.

WHAT YOU'LL NEED:

You'll need a big kettle (check thrift stores or yard sales for a throwaway), water, cornstarch, fine-grain sand, and a large plastic bowl.

FOR EXTRA IMPACT:

- Read aloud **Deuteronomy 33:19,** and ask kids how their sand-castle creations are like or unlike treasures in the sand.

- Have kids tell ways we feast on God's hidden treasures.

- Hide little plastic toys in a wading pool filled with sand. Let kids take turns finding the "treasures hidden in the sand" and then returning them for others to find.

DIRECTIONS

In the kettle, bring 4 ½ cups of water to a boil. Add 3 cups of cornstarch, and bring to a boil again. Gradually add 6 cups of sand, stirring constantly. Remove from heat. Transfer the mixture into a plastic bowl, and let it cool. This is enough clay for about a dozen kids to make small sand castles or other sculptures. Air dry the finished creations.

SAND SCULPTURES

Kids will appreciate the details God put into each of us as they create these unique paperweights.

WHAT YOU'LL NEED:

You'll need a Bible, a large bucket, a large stick, clean sand, a scoop, glue (large quantity), tempera paints, assorted beads, plastic lids, and toothpicks.

FOR EXTRA IMPACT:

- Read aloud **Psalm 139:14,** and ask kids: What do you think it means to be fearfully and wonderfully made?

- Ask: How does it feel to know that God created each one of us with special gifts? Explain.

- Have kids draw a self-portrait and write on it, "I am fearfully and wonderfully made." Then have kids find a partner, show each other their pictures, and tell about the special gifts God has given them.

DIRECTIONS

Read aloud **Psalm 139:13-16.** Say: Imagine how God worked to create the earth, and imagine how he worked on each of you.

Pour the sand into the bucket. Have kids reach into the bucket and lift out a handful of sand. Tell them to let the sand trickle through their fingers. Say: God created every single grain of sand, just as he created every one of us.

Pour glue into the sand bucket, and stir with a large stick until all the sand is moistened. Have kids choose a plastic lid to be a base for their paperweight. Scoop the sand mixture into children's hands, and let them form paperweights. They can decorate their paperweights by pressing beads into the sand or dropping small amounts of paint onto the sand and swirling it with a toothpick to add color. Kids can press their fingers or toothpicks into the sand mixture to make different shapes and textures.

Let decorated paperweights dry for one week. Kids can then peel away the plastic lid and enjoy their sand creations.

SCRATCHBOARD PICTURES

Kids learn that Jesus helps us see what's hidden.

WHAT YOU'LL NEED:

You'll need a Bible, heavy paper, pastel crayons, black poster paint in small dishes, bent paper clips or nails, dish soap, and paintbrushes.

FOR EXTRA IMPACT:

- Have several hair dryers on hand, and let kids blow dry their paintings to speed drying time.

- Have kids close their eyes while one child turns a flashlight off or on and hides it under a bowl. Then have kids guess whether the light is on or off.

- Play a game of Hide the Object with kids having to listen to the leader's clues to find the hidden object. Let the child who finds the object hide it for the next round.

DIRECTIONS

Mix a drop of soap into each small dish of black paint. Have kids color their entire paper with crayons. Tell kids to make a thick layer of crayon as they color. Then have kids paint black all over the layer of crayons. Let the paint dry. Scratch a picture into the black painted surface with a bent paper clip or nail. The beautiful colors underneath will show through!

Read aloud **Mark 4:21-23.** Ask: What do you think Jesus meant by "whatever is hidden"? How will Jesus help us see what's hidden? How was our black picture like or unlike not knowing everything Jesus wants us to know? How is our scratched picture like or unlike knowing everything Jesus wants us to know? How can we be better listeners to learn from Jesus?

SILLYETTES

Kids love making these fun self-portraits.

WHAT YOU'LL NEED:

You'll need half-sheets of poster board, tape, overhead projector, markers, glue, and various craft materials, such as feathers, fabric, paper, beads, yarn, or glitter.

FOR EXTRA IMPACT:

- Read aloud **Psalm 139:14** and ask kids: In what ways are God's works wonderful? How is that like the way God created us?

- Ask kids: Why do you think God made each one of us with different characteristics and gifts? Explain.

- Have kids tell one of their favorite characteristics or gifts. Close in prayer, thanking God that each of us is wonderfully made.

DIRECTIONS

Tape half a sheet of poster board to the wall. Place an overhead projector on the other side of the room. Have a child stand between the projector and the poster so that his or her silhouette fills the poster board. Use a marker to trace around the child's silhouette.

Write the child's name on the back of the paper, and give the child the silhouette. Kids can use craft materials to make their silhouettes into "sillyettes." When kids have finished, hang the portraits in your hallways for engaging decorations that parents will rush to see.

SNOW ANGELS

Kids love making these fun angels.

WHAT YOU'LL NEED:

You'll need large sheets of butcher paper and markers.

FOR EXTRA IMPACT:

- For a special touch, give kids craft supplies, such as yarn, sequins, wiggle eyes, ribbons, and lace, to use as they decorate their angels.

- Read aloud **Hebrews 13:2,** and ask: Do you believe angels help us today? Have you ever had an encounter with an angel? Explain.

- Have kids tell ways we can be "angels" to others through acts of kindness.

DIRECTIONS

Children can create snow angels on large sheets of butcher paper. Have a child lie on the paper, legs slightly apart. A volunteer then traces the child's outline, but not the arms or insides of the legs. Give children two markers of the same color—one to hold in each hand—and have them move their arms up and down so that they draw long arcs on the paper. Connect the leg outlines with a curve to represent the bottom of an angel's robe. Then have the children decorate their life-size angels with markers.

 ALL AGES

SPOON PUPPETS

Kids love making these fun storytelling props.

WHAT YOU'LL NEED:

You'll need a wooden spoon for each child, glue, foil, markers, cotton balls, yarn, fake fur, fabric, ribbon, and scissors.

FOR EXTRA IMPACT:

- Have kids form groups, and let each group select a Bible story, such as Shadrach, Meshach, and Abednego. Then each child can make one of the story characters, and the group can put on a puppet show for the class.

- Give kids large plastic spoons, and let each child make several different Bible characters.

- Have shoe boxes, egg cartons, and other craft supplies on hand so kids can make play sets for their puppets.

DIRECTIONS

Give each child a wooden spoon. You can even have kids bring these from home to keep the costs down.

Have kids choose a person from the Bible and draw that person's face on the oval part of the spoon. Kids can then dress the person according to what he or she would have worn.

Cotton balls or yarn can be used for beards or hair. Fake fur and fabric work for clothing. And foil makes great weapons and armor.

Once the spoon puppets are made, have kids use them to retell Bible stories.

SPRAY ART

Kids create colorful paintings.

WHAT YOU'LL NEED:

You'll need pump spray bottles, water, food coloring, a 20-foot piece of rope, clothespins, newsprint, and paint shirts.

FOR EXTRA IMPACT:

- Read aloud **Genesis 37:3,** and have kids describe what they think Joseph's colorful coat looked like.

- Help kids each cut a paper "robe" out of newsprint or a grocery sack. Let kids cut their paintings into squares and glue the squares onto their robes to make colorful coats.

- Have kids spray paint coffee filters and hang them from the ceiling when dry to create a colorful scene.

▶ DIRECTIONS

Before class, fill spray bottles with water and drops of food coloring. Shake well to mix. Tie a 20-foot piece of rope about 4 feet from the ground between two trees or poles outside. Clothespin newsprint sheets to the rope.

Have children wear paint shirts. Then have kids choose a spray bottles to spray near the top of their newsprint. Have kids use spray bottles with other colors to spray the rest of their newsprint sheets. The colored water will drip and run. Colors will mix, creating beautiful paintings.

Once a child is through with his or her painting, remove it and allow it to dry on the grass. Place another sheet of newsprint in its place, and allow another child to create a masterpiece.

STAINED-GLASS CRAFT

Kids make colorful stained-glass art.

WHAT YOU'LL NEED:

You'll need colored tissue paper, clear self-adhesive vinyl, and scissors.

FOR EXTRA IMPACT:

- Let kids use Mod Podge to glue different color tissue paper squares on the outside of clean glass jars. When dry, add votive candles to the stained-glass candle holders.

- Make stained-glass cookies. Cut shapes from refrigerated sugar-cookie dough. Cut smaller shapes inside the cookies, fill with crushed Life Savers candies, and bake.

ALLERGY ALERT
See page 10.

- Make stained-glass hearts by placing crayon shavings between sheets of wax paper. Place in a paper bag and iron to melt the crayons; then cut the cooled wax paper into a heart shape.

DIRECTIONS

Give each child two 10x10-inch pieces of clear self-adhesive vinyl. Peel the backing off the first piece and lay it down tacky side up.

Have kids tear small pieces of tissue paper and place them on the tacky side of the self-adhesive vinyl in the shape of a cross, fish, heart, or crown. When they're done, peel the backing off the second piece of self-adhesive vinyl and carefully lay it over the artwork with the tacky side down.

Cut around the shape with scissors. Kids can lightly moisten one side and stick their stained-glass art to a window.

SUMMER FUN T'S

Kids make colorful T-shirts as fun summer-memory keepsakes.

WHAT YOU'LL NEED:

You'll need a white, 100-percent cotton T-shirt for each child; washable white glue; cold-water dye; a spray bottle; thick-bristle paintbrushes; newspaper; paint shirts; and optional latex gloves.

FOR EXTRA IMPACT:

- Have kids model their T-shirts and tell about their summer memories.

- Read aloud **Ecclesiastes 3:1** and say: Summer is over, and we are entering a new season of school. Ask: What's the most exciting thing about starting a new school year?

- Have kids tell any fears they have about the upcoming school year and pray for those concerns.

DIRECTIONS

Before kids arrive, mix the dye colors according to the package instructions, and fill the spray bottles with different colors.

Have kids place several layers of newspaper inside their T-shirts. Have them use glue and simple, broad strokes to "paint" on their T-shirts a basic drawing that symbolizes their favorite thing about summer. Allow the glue to dry on the front before decorating the back of the T-shirt.

Once the glue dries completely, take the shirts outside. Have kids put on paint shirts and spray their entire T-shirts on the front and back with the dye. (You may want kids to wear latex gloves.) Allow the shirts to dry overnight, and wash the shirts according to the dye instructions to set the dye.

SWEET ANGELS

Kids make edible angel treats.

WHAT YOU'LL NEED:

You'll need refrigerated sugar-cookie dough, a knife (adult use), plastic knives, cookie sheets, access to an oven, a spatula, cooling racks, oven mitts, and nonstick spray.

ALLERGY ALERT

See page 10.

FOR EXTRA IMPACT:

- Let kids decorate cooled cookies with icing and nonpareils, or use food color pens and other specialty decorations found wherever cake decorating supplies are sold.

- Read aloud **Luke 1:8-19** as kids eat their Sweet Angels.

- Kids can make angel-cookie ornaments and decorate an angel tree for Christmas.

DIRECTIONS

Cut a ¼-inch slice of refrigerated sugar cookie dough for each child. Have kids cut their dough circles into triangles with rounded bottoms for the angels' bodies. Use the two remaining semicircles to create wings. To create the angels' heads, give each child a pinch of dough to roll into a ball and flatten.

Have kids arrange their dough in angel formations on cookie sheets, and bake according to the package directions.

SWEET SHEEP

Kids love making and eating these cute sheep.

WHAT YOU'LL NEED:

You'll need precooked chocolate muffins, vanilla icing, shredded coconut, Fruit Roll-Ups snacks, scissors, plastic knives, and paper plates.

ALLERGY ALERT

See page 10.

FOR EXTRA IMPACT:

- Have kids set their sheep on a table and talk about how each one is different. Ask kids: How is that like or unlike how we are all different?

- Read aloud **Psalm 100:3**. Ask kids: What does it mean that we are the sheep of God's pasture?

- Ask: How do you feel knowing that you belong to God? Explain.

DIRECTIONS

Have kids peel the muffin papers off the muffins and place the muffins upside down on paper plates. Have kids ice their muffins with vanilla icing, leaving the sheep's "face" on the side and the bottom plain. Sprinkle a layer of shredded coconut over the icing for wool.

Give kids each a Fruit Roll-Ups snack. Have them remove the dried fruit from the cellophane and then cut two ¼-inch ears. Stick the ears into the icing on the sides of the sheep's head. Have kids tightly roll the Roll-Ups and then cut the roll into four equal sections for legs.

Let kids enjoy eating their Sweet Sheep.

THANKFUL TURKEYS

Kids make these tasty turkey treats to remind them to give thanks to God every day.

WHAT YOU'LL NEED:

For each turkey, you'll need a red apple, colored toothpicks, small gumdrops, red licorice, a large yellow Swedish Fish candy, a large marshmallow, and black gel icing. You'll also need card stock, markers, and scissors.

ALLERGY ALERT
See page 10.

FOR EXTRA IMPACT:

- Read aloud **Psalm 118:28-29,** and ask kids: Why should we give thanks to God?

- Have kids tell things they're thankful for while eating the Thankful Turkeys.

- Close in prayer and encourage children to each give thanks to God for at least one thing.

DIRECTIONS

Have kids each set their apple on a working surface. Stick four colored toothpicks in a semicircle into the top of the apple. Spear four small gumdrops on all the toothpicks to create multicolored tail feathers.

For the turkey's head, have kids stick a toothpick into the top of the apple opposite the tail feathers. Cut a 1-inch section of red licorice and spear it lengthwise on the toothpick for the turkey's neck. Then stack one yellow Swedish Fish candy for the beak and a large marshmallow for the turkey's head on the toothpick. Use the black gel icing to dot eyes on the marshmallow.

Have kids each cut out a large feather from the card stock. Write, "Give Thanks to God!" on the feather, and attach it to the back of the turkey with a toothpick.

TOE PAINTING

Kids learn that Christ sets them free from selfishness so they can serve others.

WHAT YOU'LL NEED:

You'll need a Bible; construction paper; red, white, and blue liquid tempera paint; aluminum pie pans; newspapers; wash basins filled with water; and towels.

FOR EXTRA IMPACT:

- Have kids each paint their handprints and footprints on large sheets of paper and write, "I will use my hands and feet to serve others."

- Have kids write or draw a picture of an act of service to do during the week.

DIRECTIONS

Have girls wear pants or shorts for this activity. Pour different-colored paint into aluminum pie pans. Cover kids' work area with newspapers. Older children may enjoy creating murals together, while younger children may enjoy making individual paintings.

Have kids take off their shoes and sit by a sheet of paper. Say: Let's celebrate freedom by painting an Independence Day picture with our toes. Place your toes in the pans of paint and paint a picture on your paper.

Once kids have finished their pictures, have them wash their feet and set the pictures aside to dry.

Have kids tell about their pictures. Then say: You were all free to create whatever you wanted to—with some guidelines, such as colors to use and a topic to focus on. Let's look at another kind of freedom we Christians enjoy.

Read aloud **Galatians 5:1, 13-14.** Ask: What does the Bible say Christians are free from?

Ask: What does the Bible mean when it talks about using our freedom to serve others? How can we use our freedom in Christ to serve others this week?

WISE MEN

Kids create their own "wise men" to celebrate Christ's birth.

WHAT YOU'LL NEED:

You'll need 3 round papier-mâché craft boxes with lids (ranging in diameter from 2 to 8 inches) for each child. These are available at craft stores. You'll also need felt, scissors, yarn, glue, tempera paints, paintbrushes, and various decorations.

FOR EXTRA IMPACT:

- Bring in pictures or books showing the wise men. Have kids discuss how they were different from each other.

- Read aloud **Matthew 2:7-12**. Ask: Why do you think the wise men brought gifts to Jesus? What gifts would you bring baby Jesus today?

- Kids can fill their boxes with gold-foil-covered chocolate coins to represent the gold the wise men brought to baby Jesus.

ALLERGY ALERT
See page 10.

DIRECTIONS

Give kids each three round papier-mâché craft boxes of different sizes. Kids will stack the boxes from largest to smallest. Have them glue bottoms of the smallest and mid-size boxes to the center of the lids of the boxes just larger. Allow the glue to dry.

Kids can decorate their boxes with paint, felt, and yarn to represent the wise men. Encourage kids to be creative as they imagine what these men might've looked like on their visit to see the baby Jesus. Once decorated, allow the creations to dry completely. Kids can use their wise men as candy keepers or give them as gifts.

CRAFTS FOR

PRESCHOOL

ACCORDION BOOKS

Kids love illustrating these fun books.

WHAT YOU'LL NEED:

You'll need 8½x11-inch sheets of light-colored card stock (4 sheets for each child), glue sticks, scissors, and cardboard.

FOR EXTRA IMPACT:

- Have kids form pairs and share their books with each other.

- Make a classroom book by adding more pages. Have a section for each child with a photograph and a drawing.

- Let older kids make the book themselves by following along with you as you direct them step by step. Then have kids fill the book with their favorite Scriptures.

DIRECTIONS

For each child, create an accordion book following these instructions. On the short side of one sheet of paper, fold back a flap about ½-inch wide. Then fold the rest of the sheet in half, keeping the flap folded toward the outside. Lay the folded sheet down with the flap on top.

Repeat this process with another sheet of paper. Then set the second folded sheet on top of the first sheet, slipping the bottom unfolded edge of the second sheet under the first flap. Glue the flap down over the bottom edge. Repeat these steps two more times for an accordion book that's eight pages long.

Create a cardboard heart template that's as big as, but no bigger than, the book's folded pages. Trace this heart over the folded book's top page, keeping the folded area within the heart outline. Cut out the heart shape through all thicknesses, being careful not to cut too much of the fold.

Help children create a book with pictures of the way their family shows love to one another. Write kids' narrated words to accompany the pictures.

AMAZING ANIMALS

Kids love making these edible treats.

WHAT YOU'LL NEED:

You'll need chocolate pudding, small paper cups, chocolate cookies, resealable plastic bags, plastic spoons, and gummy animals or animal crackers.

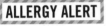

See page 10.

FOR EXTRA IMPACT:

- Let kids take turns making the sounds of their favorite animals while the others try to guess the animal.

- Paraphrase the story of Noah's ark from **Genesis 7**. Have kids put pairs of matching animals in their dirt cups.

- Fill celery sticks with cream cheese. Top the celery sticks with animal crackers.

DIRECTIONS

Have kids each fill a small paper cup ¾ full with chocolate pudding. Give each child one chocolate cookie. Have kids crush the chocolate cookies inside the resealable plastic bags. Use the chocolate cookie crumbs to create a "dirt" layer on top of the pudding layer. Insert gummy animals or animal crackers in the "dirt."

Read aloud **Genesis 1:24-25.** Have kids name as many animals as they can think of. Have kids tell which animals are their favorite and why.

ANGEL ORNAMENTS

Kids will love making these angel ornaments for Christmas.

WHAT YOU'LL NEED:

You'll need for each ornament a white or beige shoulder pad, a 25-millimeter wooden ball, a 3-inch strip of pearl beading, and a yarn loop for the hanger. You'll also need tacky glue; black and red fine-tip markers; lace; and trim such as sequins, buttons, or rickrack.

FOR EXTRA IMPACT:

- Read aloud **Psalm 148:2,** and have kids repeat the verse with you.
- Ask: How do you think the angels praise God?
- Have kids tell ways we can praise God.

DIRECTIONS

Before class, use a hot glue gun to attach a wooden ball to the top center of each shoulder pad to create the head. Glue the pearl beading strip to the top of the head for the halo. Glue the yarn loop on the angel's back for the hanger.

Have kids each decorate the face with the markers. Children can then use tacky glue to decorate the outside of the shoulder pad with the trim. Then have them bunch a strip of lace in the center and glue it to the back for wings. Allow to dry.

Overlap the two tips of each shoulder pad in the front center, and tack with a hot glue gun. Give kids their ornaments to take home.

ANGELIC MEMORIES

Kids love making these angel keepsakes.

WHAT YOU'LL NEED:

You'll need a foam paintbrush, white acrylic or tempera paint, crayons or markers, baby wipes, glue, and a black marker. You'll also need a piece of dark blue construction paper and a 2-inch white-paper circle for each child.

FOR EXTRA IMPACT:

- Take a picture of each child's face. Let kids each cut out their face and glue it onto the circle of their angel's head.

- Read aloud **Luke 2:12-14** and ask kids: Why do the angels praise God? Why do we praise God?

▶ DIRECTIONS

Have kids each place a sheet of blue paper on a table. Help children paint their right palm white and place their painted hand palm down on the paper to print the right wing of an angel. Repeat the process with the left hand. Use the baby wipes for a quick cleanup of kids' hands. Allow this part of the project to dry.

Help children paint the bottom of one foot white. Rotate the picture 180 degrees, and place the painted foot on the blue paper between the wings with the heel placed just above the handprints. Toes should point down to form a scalloped hem on the angel's robe.

When the paint is dry, have kids each glue a white paper circle at the top of the printed heel to form the angel's head. Let kids decorate the face with crayons or markers. Add the caption, "Our Little Angel" and the date.

CANDLE PUPPETS

Kids make candle puppets as a reminder that Jesus is the light of the world.

WHAT YOU'LL NEED:

You'll need a toilet-paper tube covered with yellow construction paper; small pieces of yarn; orange, yellow, and red tissue paper squares; a 1½-inch precut white poster-board flame; and two wiggle eyes for each child. You'll also need markers, glue, tape, and scissors.

FOR EXTRA IMPACT:

- Teach kids this Scripture rhyme:

    "I'm the light of the world."
    That's what Jesus said.

    With him there's no
    darkness, only light instead.

- Let kids march around the room waving their candle puppets as they say the rhyme.

- Have kids share ways we can follow Jesus' light.

DIRECTIONS

Leaving the door open for a small amount of light, turn off the lights. Ask: How would it feel to always be in the dark? Turn the light back on and ask: Does it feel better to have light? Why?

Read aloud **John 8:12.** Say: Jesus says that he is the light of the world. When we know Jesus and follow him, he brings light to our lives. Let's make candle puppets to remind us of Jesus' light in our lives.

Have kids each glue two wiggle eyes onto their toilet-paper tube. Help them draw the remainder of the face with markers and glue on yarn for the hair. Have children each scrunch the tissue-paper squares and glue them onto their poster-board flame. After children have finished, attach each flame inside the top front of the toilet-paper tube using clear tape. Then write each child's name on the back of his or her puppet.

PRESCHOOL

CARING FOR THE SPARROW

This bird-feeder craft teaches kids how great God's love is for them and his world.

WHAT YOU'LL NEED:

You'll need a Bible, oranges, knife (adult use), vegetable shortening, plastic knives, straws, yarn, scissors, and birdseed or popped popcorn.

ALLERGY ALERT
See page 10.

FOR EXTRA IMPACT:

- Show pictures of different birds, and let children describe the different characteristics. Remind kids that God made each of us special just like the birds.

- Write the words from **Matthew 10:31b**, "You are worth more than many sparrows," on sheets of paper, and let kids draw pictures of their favorite birds.

- Let kids make orange smoothies by adding the seeded orange sections to frozen vanilla yogurt or orange sherbet and then mixing in a blender.

▶ DIRECTIONS

Before kids arrive, cut oranges in half and carefully scoop out the orange sections, keeping the orange peels intact. Pierce a hole on each side of each orange half about midway between the top and bottom. Place the orange sections back in the halves.

Read aloud **Matthew 10:29-31.** Give each child an orange half, and let children eat the sections. Have them put a plastic straw through both holes in their orange half. Spread vegetable shortening inside the orange half and fill with bird seed or popped popcorn. Help kids thread a 10-inch piece of yarn through their straw and tie the yarn in a knot.

Have kids take their bird feeders home to hang in a tree. Children will see their handiwork being put to use every day as they help God care for the sparrows— and other birds.

CARING HEARTS

Kids learn how Jesus loves and cares for us.

WHAT YOU'LL NEED:

You'll need red construction paper, medium-size heart patterns, markers, scissors, tape, and a beach towel.

FOR EXTRA IMPACT:

• Kids can decorate heart-shape cookies with red icing and talk about ways we can be like Jesus and care for each other's hearts.

ALLERGY ALERT
See page 10.

• Have kids tell ways Jesus takes care of them.

• Lead kids in singing "Jesus Loves Me" as they march around the room wearing their crowns.

DIRECTIONS

Have kids each trace and cut out three to five hearts from red construction paper. Help them write their name on each heart.

Spread a beach towel on the floor, and have kids place their hearts on the towel. Have the children hold the edges of the towel. Then have the children move the towel up and down to make the hearts bounce. Encourage children not to let any of the hearts fall to the ground.

Ask: Was it easy to keep the hearts on the blanket? Why or why not? Say: We are careful with these hearts; we don't want any of them to fall. In the same way, Jesus is careful with our hearts. He loves us, and he takes care of us.

Help children find their hearts on the blanket. Then write on their hearts sayings such as "Jesus loves me" or "Jesus takes care of me." Tape a 2-inch-wide strip of red construction paper to make a crown for each child. Have children tape their hearts to their crowns, and let children wear the crowns home.

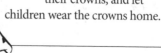

COAT FACTORY

Kids learn about Jesus' triumphant entry into Jerusalem.

WHAT YOU'LL NEED:

You'll need a Bible, newsprint, markers, crayons, green construction paper, and stickers.

FOR EXTRA IMPACT:

- Have kids sit in a circle and roll a ball back and forth. The child who catches the ball should tell something special about another child and then roll the ball to that child while children wave their palm branches and yell "[Child's name] is special!"

- Teach kids the words to this rhyme: Hosanna! Hosanna! Bless him we say. We praise the Lord Jesus on this day.

- Have kids bring in their old coats to donate to a local shelter. Let kids color greeting cards to give with the coats to tell recipients that Jesus loves them.

DIRECTIONS

Give each child a 2 ½-foot length of newsprint with the long sides folded to the middle. Have kids decorate their coats with markers, crayons, and stickers. As they're working, cut rounded necklines and armholes in each coat. When finished, let kids tear simple palm branches from the green construction paper.

Have kids wear their coats, hold their palm branches, and sit in a circle.

Paraphrase **Mark 11:1-10.** Have kids try out the praise words used in your text by shouting them several times. Designate one area of the room as "Jerusalem." Retell the story with the kids acting it out.

CREATION STICKY PICTURE

Kids learn about the Creation story with this fun interactive project.

WHAT YOU'LL NEED:

You'll need clear Con-Tact paper; transparent tape; sand; leaves; star confetti or small shiny star shapes; small, colorful feathers; pictures of animals; a picture of each child in the class; and small squares of soft material, fabric fur, shiny yellow paper, and light blue paper.

FOR EXTRA IMPACT:

- Have kids tell which part of their creation collage they like the best and why.
- Print a copy of the Creation story for each child to take home.

DIRECTIONS

Before class cut out two large matching squares of Con-Tact paper for each child. Tape all four corners of one sheet, sticky side up, to the table. Reserve the matching square for the end of the project.

Tell the following Creation story, and give kids the related objects. Have kids stick the objects anywhere on the Con-Tact paper in front of them.

Say: Once, there was nothing, then God made light (shiny yellow square). On the second day, God made the sky (light blue paper).

On the third day, God made land and dirt (sand). He also made water into seas or lakes. Then God made plants and fruit (leaf).

On the fourth day, God made the stars, the moon, and the sun (shiny stars). On the fifth day, God made birds and fish and all their friends (feather).

On the sixth day, God made animals. Some were furry, (fur fabric) and all were very special (animal picture)! On this day, God also made people like you and me. (Give each child the picture of him- or herself.)

On the seventh day, God didn't make anything! He wanted to rest and give us a day to rest (soft material).

Cover the top of each picture with the matching sheet of Con-Tact paper, sticky side down.

DID YOU EVER SEE...?

Kids learn about Jesus healing a blind man.

WHAT YOU'LL NEED:

You'll need a Bible, paper plates, and Crayola Color Changeables markers.

FOR EXTRA IMPACT:

- Have half the kids walk around the room pretending to be swaying trees, while the other kids look through pieces of waxed paper. Remove the wax paper and yell "I can see clearly." Switch roles.

- Let kids make an obstacle course using only soft items. Have kids form pairs, with one child wearing a blindfold while the other child carefully leads the partner around the course.

DIRECTIONS

Tell kids the story of the blind man at Bethsaida from **Mark 8:22-26.** Talk about how thankful the man must've been to be able to see after Jesus healed him.

Distribute paper plates and Crayola Color Changeables markers. Have children scribble a large blotch of a single color in the middle of the paper plate. Then have them take turns using the "color changer" marker to draw a picture of something they're thankful for that God has made.

Have kids hold up their paper plates as you lead them in singing this song to the tune of "Did You Ever See a Lassie?":

Have you ever seen a [name of picture on plate]? (Children cover their eyes.)

A [name of picture]? A [name of picture]?

Have you ever seen a [name of picture]?

And the blind man said, "Yes!" (Children uncover eyes and shout "yes!")

Repeat the song with each child's picture. Then make a bulletin-board display with the paper plates, or hang them from the ceiling with colored yarn.

EDIBLE HEART ART

Kids will love creating and eating these yummy masterpieces.

WHAT YOU'LL NEED:

You'll need a heart-shaped cookie "canvas," 2 small paper cups, a sheet of wax paper, and pudding "paint" for each child. For approximately 12 children, you'll need a 15-ounce package of ready-made pie crust for the canvas and a 3.4-ounce box of vanilla instant pudding for the paint. You'll also need red food coloring and a large heart-shaped cookie cutter.

ALLERGY ALERT
See page 10.

FOR EXTRA IMPACT:

- Let kids fingerpaint on wax paper with leftover pudding.

- Have an art show, and let kids show off their creations before eating them.

- Read aloud **Proverbs 15:30,** and have kids tell things that bring joy to their hearts.

DIRECTIONS

Before class, cut out a heart-shaped cookie "canvas" from the pie crust for each child. Bake the hearts according to package directions. To make the paint, prepare the pudding according to package directions. After the pudding is set, place two tablespoons of pudding in each cup (two for each child). Add eight drops of red food coloring to one cup, four drops to the other, and mix each one thoroughly. Keep refrigerated until ready to use.

Give children paint cups and a cookie canvas on a sheet of wax paper. Let children fingerpaint on the "canvases" and then eat the yummy treats.

FAITH IN BLOOM

Kids make these photo keepsakes for Valentine's Day gifts.

WHAT YOU'LL NEED:

For each child, you'll need 5 small heart cutouts, a 3-inch poster-board circle, a green chenille wire, a 3-inch terra-cotta flower pot, and a plastic-foam ball that fits in the pot. You'll also need shredded green paper, a red permanent marker, glue, and a wallet-size photo of each child.

FOR EXTRA IMPACT:

- Have kids name people who have helped their faith grow. Let kids decide who they want to give their blooming photo flower to for Valentine's Day.

- Read aloud **2 Thessalonians 1:3,** and have kids tell ways our faith grows.

- Ask kids why they think it's important for our faith to grow.

▶ DIRECTIONS

Have kids each place the hearts in a circle and glue the bottom tips to the edge of the poster board circle. Then place one end of the chenille wire on the circle and glue their photo on top, securing the wire between the photo and the circle. Place the Styrofoam ball in the bottom of the terra-cotta pot. Then stick the other end of the chenille wire into the foam. Fill the remainder of the pot with shredded green paper. With the red permanent marker, write on each child's pot, "Thanks for helping my faith bloom! Happy Valentine's Day!"

FEELING BAG-BOOKS

Teach kids about feelings with this fun book.

WHAT YOU'LL NEED:

You'll need 7 large paper grocery bags, markers, hole punch, ribbon, scissors, 6 large Ziploc bags, and items such as confetti, colored paper, crayons, gum, small candies, balloons, and tissues.

ALLERGY ALERT

See page 10.

FOR EXTRA IMPACT:

- Have kids make individual Feeling Bag-Books using paper lunch bags and small resealable plastic bags.

- Have kids color faces depicting four feelings on paper plates. Using a hole punch and ribbon, tie the plates together at the top.

DIRECTIONS

Lay a paper bag on a flat surface with the folded bottom down. Write "God Made Feelings" across the bag, starting at the closed end of the bag and writing toward the open end of the bag.

Choose six feelings that the group would like to make a book about. Write each feeling on a different bag. Starting at the closed end of the bag and writing toward the open end of the bag, write in this form: I feel angry when... or, I feel happy when...

Lay your bags on top of each other and punch two holes in the closed ends of the bags about 1 inch from the edge and 3 inches apart. Cut an 8-inch piece of ribbon and thread it through the holes. Tie a bow in the ribbon on the title side.

Say: Look through these items and choose things that represent these feelings. For example, you may choose a balloon and confetti for when you're happy. Put the "feeling" items together in a Ziploc bag and put it in the paper bag with that feeling.

Read aloud the paper-bag book. As you read each feeling, take out the plastic bag and let children tell why they chose their items.

GOD MADE FEELINGS
HAPPY
I feel happy when...

FOOTPRINTS KEEPSAKE

Kids can make this special keepsake for Mother's Day or Father's Day.

WHAT YOU'LL NEED:

You'll need an 8½x11-inch copy of "My Footprints" (on this page) for each child, washable paint, ribbon, and a water basin and towels for cleanup.

FOR EXTRA IMPACT:

- Provide banner paper, and have each child make a set of footprints on it. As kids look at the footprints, talk about how God made each one of us different.

- Write on the banner "Our footprints follow Jesus." Then display it on the wall.

- Read aloud **Luke 18:22,** and have kids tell ways we can follow Jesus.

DIRECTIONS

Give each child a copy of "My Footprints." Help children make washable-paint footprints on their poems. When footprints have dried, write each child's name on his or her poem, roll the paper like a scroll, and tie with a ribbon.

My Footprints

When I was just a baby,
My footprints were real small.
I could not walk anywhere.
You carried me proud and tall.

Now that I am bigger,
My footprints are big, too.
I can run, walk, gallop, skip;
But I still need you.

I need your guidance and your love
To keep my footprints placed
On paths where I will learn what's right
And seek God's love and grace.

Some day when I grow up,
I hope you will look back
To think of times when I was small
And be proud of my feet's path.

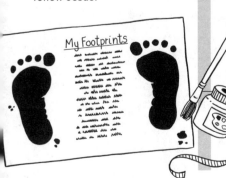

GLITTER JARS

These glittery globes will remind kids of the goodness of God's creation.

WHAT YOU'LL NEED:

You'll need a Bible, baby food jars with lids, small artificial flower blossoms, clay, glitter, and nail polish.

FOR EXTRA IMPACT:

- For added sparkle, have kids add foil confetti to the jars.

- For a fun, ocean-like effect, add a couple drops of blue food coloring to the jars.

- Teach kids this prayer to say as they shake their jars:

  Thank you, God, for the world you made. May I see your goodness every day.

DIRECTIONS

Have kids press clay onto the inside of a baby-food jar lid and stick artificial flower blossoms into the clay. Have kids fill the jars almost to the top with water and drop in a few pinches of glitter. Screw the lids onto the jars, and paint around the edges of the lids with nail polish to seal the lids. Allow to dry. Have kids shake the jars and then set them on the lid.

As the glitter swirls around in the water, ask: How did you feel as you made your small world that glitters? How do you think God felt when he made the world?

Read aloud **Genesis 1:31.** Say: God saw all that he had made, and it was good. What do you think is good about your jar? What do you think about God's creation?

GLUE AND GLITTER BUTTERFLIES

Kids learn about becoming new creations in Christ.

WHAT YOU'LL NEED:

You'll need a Bible, glue, wax paper, glitter, box lid, nylon filament thread, and tacks.

FOR EXTRA IMPACT:

- Let kids crouch down on the floor and pretend to be caterpillars and then pop up and flutter around the room like butterflies, shouting, "I'm a new creation in Christ."

- Let kids make a small butterfly to take home. Place double-stick tape around the edges of precut construction-paper butterfly shapes. Let kids sprinkle on glitter and add chenille wires for the antennae.

- Kids can make several small butterflies and tie them on a coat hanger with yarn for a flowing mobile.

DIRECTIONS

Help kids "paint" a simple butterfly shape on a sheet of wax paper with the glue. Be sure that each butterfly body is filled in with glue. Help kids make the outline of the wing sections at least ½ inch thick.

Shake assorted colors of glitter over the glue, making sure the glue is completely covered. Gently lift the wax paper, and shake the excess glitter back into the glitter container or a box lid for future use.

Set the wax paper aside for several days to let the glue and glitter dry. When it's completely dry, carefully peel the butterfly shape from the paper.

Help kids thread a length of nylon filament thread through each butterfly. Hang the butterflies from the ceiling where they can blow in the breeze!

Read aloud **2 Corinthians 5:17.** Say: When a caterpillar becomes a butterfly, it is a new creation. The Bible says when we are in Christ, we become new creations. Ask: What is one thing about you that shows that you are a new creation in Christ?

Close in prayer, thanking God for the new life that's available through Jesus' death and resurrection.

I CAN PRAY

Kids learn about prayer.

WHAT YOU'LL NEED:

You'll need construction paper, stickers, glitter, crayons, and empty plastic powdered-drink canisters. Remove the labels from the canisters.

FOR EXTRA IMPACT:

- Have kids form pairs, share their drawings with each other, and pray together by saying a simple prayer, such as, "Help us, God."

- Challenge kids to take their canisters home and pray for their requests every day.

- Let kids make another canister to fill with paper strips on which they've drawn things they're thankful for. Encourage kids to use these to give thanks to God every day.

DIRECTIONS

Give each child a plastic canister that you've covered with construction paper. On each can, write, "I CAN Pray." Have kids decorate their cans with stickers, glitter, and crayons.

Give each child four small pieces of paper. Have kids each draw a picture of something they want to pray for on each paper. Suggest praying for Mommy, Daddy, your church, and people who are sick. Have kids fold their drawings and put them into their cans. During prayer time, have kids pull out pictures and pray for what they've drawn.

PRESCHOOL

INCREDIBLE EDIBLE SCULPTURE

Kids will have fun making edible sculptures and learning how God made each of us different.

WHAT YOU'LL NEED:

You'll need resealable plastic bags, cream cheese, honey, nonfat dry milk, paper plates, M&M'S candies, mini-marshmallows, red shoestring licorice, and shredded coconut.

ALLERGY ALERT

See page 10.

FOR EXTRA IMPACT:

- Have kids sit in a circle and share something special about the child to their right.

- Take photos of the kids with their sculptures to put on a bulletin board in your room for a festive display.

- Give kids a copy of the rhyme to take home and do the fingerplay with their families.

DIRECTIONS

Fill a resealable plastic bag with a 8 ounces of cream cheese, ½ cup nonfat dry milk, and 1 tablespoon honey. Seal the bag, and squeeze it to mix the ingredients until smooth. One bag will supply enough dough for 5 kids.

Storage: Unused portions must be stored in an airtight container and kept refrigerated. Because cream cheese is perishable, use the expiration date on the cream cheese package as your guide for how long you can keep this play dough.

Give each child a small ball of this edible dough on a paper plate. Have each child knead the dough, press it into a circle, and then make a face using M&M'S candies and mini marshmallows for the eyes and nose, red shoestring licorice for the mouth, and shredded coconut for the hair.

Before kids eat their sculptures, have them walk around the room and look at each other's creations. Ask: Do you see any two sculptures that look exactly alike? Does God make any two people exactly alike?

Lead kids in the words and actions to this rhyme:

God made you. (Point to someone.)

God made me. (Point to yourself.)

We're all different (Point to everyone.)

In God's family. (Point up and then cross your arms over your chest.)

LIFESAVERS

Kids learn that Jesus is their lifesaver.

WHAT YOU'LL NEED:

You'll need a Bible, yellow poster board, scissors, sand, powdered tempera paint, glue, seashells, and chairs.

FOR EXTRA IMPACT:

- Let kids share about things that makes them afraid. Have the other kids respond by shouting, "Don't be afraid! Jesus is with you!"

- Have kids pray to thank Jesus for always being with us so we never have to be afraid.

- Print, "Jesus is my lifesaver!" on large index cards. Let kids tape miniature rolls of Life Savers candies onto the cards to take home as reminders that Jesus is always there.

DIRECTIONS

Before class, cut yellow poster-board circles approximately 24 inches in diameter. You'll need one for each child. Cut out the center of the circle so it's large enough to fit around a child's waist. Slice the circle to make an opening. Make colored sand by adding dry tempera paint to sand.

Have kids each decorate a "lifesaver" by "painting" glue on a poster-board circle and sprinkling it with colored sand. Kids can glue on small seashells.

Then gather children and say: We're going to take a boat ride. To help keep us safe, we need to put on our lifesavers. Lifesavers help us float if we fall into the water.

Use chairs to form a boat. Have kids sit in the boat. Read aloud **Matthew 8:23-27.** Have kids act out sea motions by waving their arms and make wind sounds by rubbing their hands together and blowing through their mouths.

Ask: Why were Jesus' friends afraid? Have you ever been afraid? Why or why not? How would you have felt if you were in the boat with Jesus? How do you think Jesus' friends felt when the boat stopped rocking?

Say: With Jesus, we don't have to be afraid because he's always with us.

MALLOW SHEEP

Kids have fun making edible sheep.

WHAT YOU'LL NEED:

You'll need large and miniature marshmallows, white frosting, red shoestring licorice, Red Hots candies, plastic knives, and paper plates.

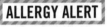
ALLERGY ALERT
See page 10.

FOR EXTRA IMPACT:

- Read aloud **Luke 15:3-7,** and let kids act out the story. Have kids take turns being the lost sheep and the shepherd.

- Have kids that have lost a pet and then found it tell how the experience felt and why.

- Read aloud **Psalm 23,** and ask kids: In what ways is God our shepherd? How can we follow him?

DIRECTIONS

Give each child two large marshmallows for the sheep's body and one marshmallow for the head. Use miniature marshmallows for legs and a tail. Cut one miniature marshmallow in half vertically, and place one half on each side of the sheep's head for ears.

Use frosting to connect all the marshmallows. Create the sheep's eyes and mouth using Red Hots candies and shoestring licorice, attached with frosting.

MOTHER HELPERS

Kids learn about helping their mothers just as Miriam did.

WHAT YOU'LL NEED:

You'll need a Bible, white construction paper, tempera paint, paintbrushes, Con-Tact paper, a hair dryer, a pancake turner, a fabric softener lid, cookie cutters, a small whisk, a sponge, and an old toothbrush.

FOR EXTRA IMPACT:

- Challenge kids to find one thing they can do every day to help their mothers.

- Let kids make a play area to act out the story of Miriam watching Moses from the bulrushes. Use a blue blanket for the water, leafy potted plants for reeds, and a doll in a basket for the baby.

- Have kids play Mother Says instead of Simon Says. Use commands such as "Mother says make your bed," or "Wash the dishes," and have kids pretend to make their beds and wash dishes.

DIRECTIONS

Give kids each a sheet of white construction paper. Have them use tempera paint to make prints on their paper with a pancake turner, a fabric softener lid, cookie cutters, a small whisk, a sponge, and an old toothbrush. Allow the papers to dry.

Ask: How can you use each item to help your mother? What other ways do you help your mother? Say: Let's hear a story about how Miriam helped her mother.

Paraphrase **Exodus 2:1-10** to tell the story of Moses' sister Miriam watching baby Moses from the reeds. Ask: What did Miriam do to help her mother? How do you think Miriam felt as she helped her mother? How do you feel when you help your mother?

At the end of class, use a hair dryer to finish drying any wet paint. Then cover the papers with clear Con-Tact paper so kids can give them to their mothers as place mats.

PHOTO BOUQUETS

Kids make treasured photo keepsakes.

WHAT YOU'LL NEED:

You'll need 6 photos of each child, poster board, tape, glue, scissors, craft sticks painted green, pots, and floral foam.

FOR EXTRA IMPACT:

- Let kids decorate terra-cotta pots with paint and ribbon to hold their photo bouquets.

- Read aloud **Proverbs 18:16,** and have kids tell why we give gifts.

- Have kids share how it feels to receive gifts and how it feels to give gifts to others.

DIRECTIONS

Help kids create gifts for their parents and grandparents that'll be treasured for years. Ahead of time, take six photos of each child so you can have them printed for this craft. Or have kids bring in six photos of themselves that you can cut up.

From poster board, cut out flower and leaf shapes. Have kids cut out their pictures and glue them to the center of their flowers. Then use tape on the back of the flowers and leaves to attach them to green wooden sticks. Kids can then arrange their flowers in small pots with floral foam in the bottom.

PRAISE KAZOOS

Kids make praise instruments to show their love for Jesus.

WHAT YOU'LL NEED:

You'll need toilet-paper tubes, rubber bands, 4-inch squares of wax paper, and a straightened paper clip.

FOR EXTRA IMPACT:

- Read aloud **Psalm 150:3,** and ask kids: How do you think Jesus feels when we praise him?

- Let kids decorate their kazoos with markers and streamers.

- Have a praise parade, and let kids march around and play their kazoos

DIRECTIONS

Give each child a toilet-paper tube, a rubber band, and a 4-inch square of wax paper. Use the rubber band to hold the wax paper on one end of the tube. Use the paper clip to poke holes in the wax paper. Have kids put the open end of the tube to their lips and rehearse by singing these words to the tune of "Yankee Doodle."

Verse: *Jesus Christ, he came to town, a-riding on a donkey. Jesus came to be my King, and that is why I'm singing.*

Chorus: *Jesus Christ came to town, came to be my Savior. Jesus Christ came to town. I'm so glad he loves me!*

RAINDROPS AND MUD PLOPS

Kids learn about how rain helps plants grow.

WHAT YOU'LL NEED:

You'll need brown finger paint, blue construction paper, markers, scissors, and glue. You'll also need to copy the poem onto 8½x11 white paper for each child.

FOR EXTRA IMPACT:

- Read the poem aloud, and ask kids how they feel when it's stormy.
- Ask: What can you do when you're afraid?
- Close in prayer, thanking God for the rain and asking him to help children remember not to be afraid during storms.

DIRECTIONS

Before kids arrive, copy this poem for each child:

When the lightning strikes

and the thunder roars,

Don't be afraid,

but go quickly indoors.

For it is God's plan, you see,

Not to scare or frighten me.

The plants need water—just like me!

Have kids use brown finger paint to make muddy fingerprints on the bottom of their paper. While the fingerprints dry, have kids cut out large blue raindrops and glue them around the poem. Then use markers to color flowers on top of the dry fingerprints.

Discuss how rain helps plants grow. Then brainstorm about other ways rain is helpful.

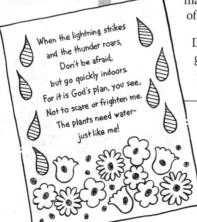

When the lightning strikes and the thunder roars, Don't be afraid, but go quickly indoors. For it is God's plan, you see, Not to scare or frighten me. The plants need water— just like me!

SWEET BIBLE SNACK

Kids make snacks to remind them that God's Word is sweet.

WHAT YOU'LL NEED:

You'll need napkins, paper plates, plastic knives, graham crackers, white frosting, black and red sprinkles, red shoe-string licorice, and a Bible that shows Jesus' words in red.

ALLERGY ALERT
See page 10.

FOR EXTRA IMPACT:

- Lead kids in singing a round of "The B-I-B-L-E" before they eat their Sweet Bible Snack.

- Read aloud **Matthew 4:2-4,** and ask: How can our hearts be fed by God's Word?

- Before kids eat, have them say a blessing to thank God for his Word and for the Sweet Bible Snacks.

DIRECTIONS

Say: The Bible is a special book because God talks to us through the Bible.

Open your Bible to one of the gospels, show kids the passage, and say: The Bible says that God's promises are sweet to us. Most of the words in the Bible are black, but Jesus' words are red.

Give each child a paper plate and napkin. Help kids spread frosting on graham crackers. Then have kids put black and red sprinkles on top. Have them add licorice bookmarks to the middle of their Bible snacks.

Say: The black sprinkles remind us of words in the Bible, and the red sprinkles remind us of Jesus' words in red. Let's thank God for this sweet snack that reminds us of how good the Bible is. Then let's eat!

VALENTINE FAN

Kids will love these handmade creations for Mom and Dad!

WHAT YOU'LL NEED:

You'll need plain paper, marker, contruction paper, white card stock, red and pink crayons, stapler, pink or red tempera paint, dish soap, sponges, jumbo craft sticks, dishpan of warm water, and towels.

FOR EXTRA IMPACT:

- Let kids march around the room to music while waving their valentine fans.

- Have kids tell about special people they love.

- Teach kids this rhyme:

  Jesus loves you; yes, it's true.

  Jesus loves you, and I do, too!

DIRECTIONS

At the top of a sheet of paper, draw a heart outline and write, "Jesus loves you!" in it. At the top of another sheet of paper, draw a heart outline and write, "I love you, too!" in it. Write your church name and the date at the bottom of this second paper. For each child, photocopy each paper onto white card stock.

Have kids color their valentines with red and pink crayons. Print each child's name just above the date.

Mix pink or red tempera paint with liquid dish soap for easy cleanup. Spread paint on a sponge. Lay out each child's valentine face up. Have kids each press their hand into the paint on the sponge and then make a handprint on each card. Re-apply paint between handprints. Messy hands can go right into a dishpan of warm water that you've set on a thick towel.

After the paint has dried, place the two sheets of card stock back to back, and staple them together at the top edges. Staple a jumbo craft-stick "handle" between the papers at the bottom, and glue the edges together.

BACK

THE BEST OF

children's ministry
MAGAZINE

CRAFTS FOR

UPPER ELEMENTARY

BEARING FRUIT

Kids make encouraging cards for their dads.

WHAT YOU'LL NEED:

You'll need a Bible, packets of fruit or vegetable seeds, construction paper, markers, and glue.

FOR EXTRA IMPACT:

- Tape the seed packets to the cards instead of gluing them, and encourage kids to plant the seeds at home with their dads.

- Let kids make a colorful classroom bulletin board. Write, "We plant seeds for Jesus," and decorate with seed packets and construction-paper flowers. For added pizazz, glue a picture of each child in the center of each flower.

- Read aloud **Galatians 5:22-23,** and let kids choose one fruit of the Spirit and share one way they can show that quality to others.

DIRECTIONS

Give each child a packet of fruit or vegetable seeds and a sheet of construction paper. Ask a child to read aloud **Galatians 5:22-23** about the fruit of the Spirit. Talk about these Scriptures as the children fold their papers in half to make cards.

On the front page of the cards, kids can write, "Dad, you plant the seeds. . ." Inside the cards on the right-hand side, have children glue their seed packets and write, ". . . that'll help me bear fruit for Jesus." On the inside left-hand page of each card, have kids write the words from **Galatians 5:22-23.** Then have kids sign their cards. Dads will treasure this encouraging card.

UPPER ELEMENTARY

BIBLE FISH

Kids make a colorful display of the
Easter story.

WHAT YOU'LL NEED:

You'll need an even number
of large, precut paper fish
shapes (at least one per child),
stapler, tissue paper, markers,
construction paper, glue,
sticker name tags, yarn, and
various craft supplies.

FOR EXTRA IMPACT:

- Let pairs read their Bible
  passage aloud and show
  their fish to the class.

- Hang the fish in order of
  the passages, and attach
  the Scripture verses for a
  chronological display of the
  Easter story.

DIRECTIONS

Before kids arrive, print these portions
of the Easter story on paper: Jesus' arrest
(**Luke 22:47-54**); Jesus before Pilate (**Luke
23:1-7**); Jesus before Herod (**Luke 23:8-25**);
Simon bears the cross (**Luke 23:26-31**); the
Crucifixion (**Luke 23:33-49**); Jesus' burial
(**Luke 23:50-56**); the Resurrection (**Luke
24:1-12**); the road to Emmaus (**Luke 24:13-
35**); and the Ascension (**Luke 24:50-53**).

Have kids work with a partner. Give each
pair one Bible passage. Have pairs read the
verses and decide how they can decorate
their fish to illustrate this part of Easter.

Have kids use the craft materials to
decorate their fish. Then they can sign a
name tag and stick it on their fish to show
who did the great artwork. Have kids staple
both sides of their fish together, leaving
an opening, stuff tissue paper through the
opening, and then staple the fish shut.

Afterward, use yarn to hang the fish from
your classroom ceiling for everyone to enjoy.

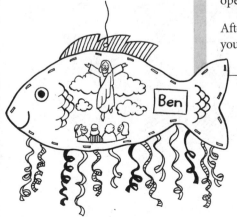

UPPER ELEMENTARY

CHURCH MOUSE PADS

Kids can design their own mouse pads with this quick and easy activity.

WHAT YOU'LL NEED:

You'll need 9x7½-inch sheets of craft foam in assorted colors, 9x7½-inch sheets of sticky-back craft foam, pencils, and scissors.

FOR EXTRA IMPACT:

- Bring in pictures of Christian symbols for kids to see. Explain what the different symbols mean.
- Have kids each show the class their mouse pad, tell why they picked that symbol, and say what it means to them.
- Let kids use markers or paint pens to write their favorite Scripture verses on their mouse pads.

DIRECTIONS

Give each child a sheet of sticky-back craft foam. Have kids choose a sheet of any color plain craft foam.

Have kids cut out a Christian symbol, such as a cross, fish, crown, or heart, from a third piece of plain craft foam. The symbol must fit inside the 9x7½-inch sheet of craft foam.

Have kids trace the symbol onto the craft foam and then carefully cut it out. Kids can press the cutout into the stencil, creating a contrasting design. Have kids peel the backing off the sticky-back craft foam and then carefully place the sticky side on the bottom of the craft foam design, matching the edges.

FATHER'S DAY HOUSE

Kids make paper houses with special treats for their fathers or special adult males in their lives.

WHAT YOU'LL NEED:

You'll need 8½x11 sheets of white card stock, 3x3-inch resealable bags, scissors, double-sided tape, crayons, markers, large stickers, and small candies.

ALLERGY ALERT

See page 10.

FOR EXTRA IMPACT:

- Have kids tell ways we can serve the Lord.
- Read aloud **Exodus 20:12**, and ask kids what it means to "honor your father."
- Challenge kids to pick one thing to do during the week to honor their dads.

DIRECTIONS

Before you begin, draw the diagram on a sheet of card stock, carefully following the dimensions listed. (See illustration.) Write the words and reference from **Joshua 24:15** on each door to the right of the doorknob. Photocopy the diagram onto card stock. Each sheet of card stock makes two houses. Cut the card stock in half along the solid center lines. Make a model house for children to see.

Have kids turn the card stock face down and fold back along the dotted lines. Tell kids to set the house on its base, and fold the top flap over the back flap. Then unfold. Use markers and crayons to decorate the front of the house.

Have kids fill a resealable bag with small candies and close it. Using double-sided tape, attach the bag to the inside of the house just below the top fold. Re-fold the top flap, and secure it to the back flap with a large sticker.

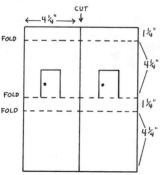

(105)

FISHER OF MEN PIN

Kids can share their faith with their friends with this creative craft.

WHAT YOU'LL NEED:

You'll need a Bible, scissors, extra-fine-tip black permanent markers, and thick tacky or craft-foam glue. For each pin, you'll need a 1x3½-inch strip of craft foam, any color; a 2-inch square of white craft foam; and a 1½-inch jewelry pin attachment.

FOR EXTRA IMPACT:

- Cut cardboard patterns of banners and hooks for kids to trace on the craft foam.

- Give each child a piece of netting. Have kids cut people shapes out of the craft foam to glue onto the netting and then attach a paper tag to the net with the words, "I'm a fisher of men for Jesus."

- Have kids list ways they can share their faith with their friends during the following week, using the pins as conversation-starters. Have kids report back the next week with their faith-sharing stories.

DIRECTIONS

Have kids cut banners out of the colored craft foam and cut hook shapes from the white craft foam. Glue the hook on the pointed end of the banner shape. Help kids write "Fisher of Men" down the length of the banner. Glue the pin to the back of the banner. Allow the glue to dry before wearing.

Read aloud **Matthew 4:18-20.** Ask: What does it mean to be fishers of men? What are ways we can follow Jesus?

Close in prayer asking Jesus to help kids share their faith with others so they can be fishers of men like Peter and Andrew.

UPPER ELEMENTARY

GOOD NEWS TULIPS

Kids make tulips as a reminder that Jesus is always with us.

WHAT YOU'LL NEED:

You'll need precut 4x5-inch pieces of red, pink, blue, and white felt; glue; ribbon; glitter; scissors; staplers; green bumpy chenille wires; plastic sandwich baggies; mixed dried fruit; yellow paper strips; and fine-tip permanent markers.

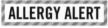

ALLERGY ALERT

See page 10.

FOR EXTRA IMPACT:

- Reread aloud **Matthew 28:20,** and ask: How does it feel to know Jesus is with us always?

- Have kids pray by name for the person they will give their Good News Tulip to and ask God to help them always feel Jesus' presence.

DIRECTIONS

Read aloud **Matthew 28:1-8.** Say: It may have been dark inside the tomb, but it really was a place of great joy! Have kids layer three 4x5-inch pieces of the same color felt and cut the layers into a 4-inch-tall and 3-inch-wide egg shape. Have kids take the top egg off the stack and staple the two stacked pieces along the right edge, leaving the top one quarter open, as shown in the illustration.

Fold both pieces in half toward the stapled outer edge. Lay the third piece on top of the other two, matching the open edges, and staple. Again leave the top one quarter open. The triangle of egg shapes forms a tulip bud. Trim the bottom of the tulip to get it to stand up.

Decorate the outside of the tulip with glitter and ribbon. Form leaves at the base with green bumpy chenille wires.

As the glue dries, fill baggies with dried fruit and tie the baggies with ribbons. Place them inside the tulips. Write, " 'I am with you always'—Matthew 28:20" on the yellow paper strips, and place them inside the tulips. Have children deliver their Good News Tulips to friends and neighbors.

HARVEST CROSS

Kids make a harvest cross to mark the changing seasons.

WHAT YOU'LL NEED:

You'll need a Bible, 10 small or medium pine cones per child, dried or artificial fall leaves, ribbon, craft wire, cardboard, scissors, a hot glue gun, and craft glue.

FOR EXTRA IMPACT:

- Have kids write, "'There is a time for everything, and a season for every activity under heaven'—Ecclesiastes 3:1" on a tag and attach it to the cross hanger.

- Ask kids: What's most special to you about this season? What can we enjoy and thank God for at this time of year?

- Have kids bring in old school photos from different years to display on a classroom bulletin board. As kids look at the photos, talk about how people change just as seasons do.

DIRECTIONS

Read aloud **Ecclesiastes 3:1-8.** Ask: Why do you think God made seasons? How do our lives change like the seasons? To celebrate this season, we're going to make a harvest cross.

Cut out a cardboard cross for each child to use as backing. Adults will need to help with this next step. Using a hot glue gun, glue the pine cones to the cardboard backing with the pointed ends up. Allow the glue to cool.

Have kids use craft glue to affix the dried or artificial leaves to the central part of the cross. Have kids tie a ribbon bow and glue it on top of the leaf arrangement. Finally, kids can make a wire loop for a hanger. Have adults affix the hangers with hot glue.

HEART FULL OF KISSES

Kids make special Valentines to say thanks to those who minister to them.

WHAT YOU'LL NEED:

You'll need 8½x11-inch pieces of red felt (2 for each child), another color of felt, glue, scissors, pencils, Hershey's Kisses chocolates, and note cards.

ALLERGY ALERT
See page 10.

FOR EXTRA IMPACT:

- Have kids sit in a circle and place the leftover Hershey's Kisses chocolates in the middle. As kids tell ways they can touch someone's heart, let them get a chocolate for each way they name.

- Read aloud **Philippians 1:3.** Have kids name people they're thankful for and say why.

- Have kids pray and thank God for each person named.

DIRECTIONS

Have kids stack two pieces of 8½x11 red felt. Fold one felt piece in half, then draw one half of a heart along the fold, making it as large as will fit on the felt. Cut out the heart. Cut the second piece of felt in the same way.

Outline the border of one heart with glue, leaving a 3-inch section at the top dry. Lay the second heart on top of the first, matching the edges. Have kids outline one hand on a piece of different color felt and cut it out. Attach the felt hand to the heart with glue.

Once the glue is dry, use puffy fabric paint to write "You touch my heart" on the side without the hand.

Fill the heart with Hershey's Kisses chocolates. Write the words of **Philippians 1:3** on a note card, and put it in the heart. Kids can deliver the hearts to Sunday school teachers, volunteers, or children's ministers.

JONAH AND THE RAGING SEA

Kids will love this interactive craft project.

WHAT YOU'LL NEED:

You'll need a Bible, empty plastic 2-liter bottles with lids, water, green and blue food coloring, vegetable oil, measuring cup, plastic margarine tub lids, scissors, permanent markers, aluminum foil, small seashells, glue, and tape.

FOR EXTRA IMPACT:

- Use clear nail polish to paint around the edges of the lid instead of using tape and glue. Allow to dry for a quick seamless seal.

- Have kids form groups of two and take turns using their sea bottles to tell the story of Jonah to each other.

- Have kids sit in a circle, place a sea bottle in the middle, and take turns spinning the bottle. When the bottle stops, let the child it "lands" on roll into the middle of the circle as if being tossed by the waves and yell, "Lord save us from the raging sea."

DIRECTIONS

Before class, use warm water to remove labels from bottles. Have kids each fill their plastic bottle about two-thirds full of water. Add a few drops of food coloring and ¼ cup of vegetable oil. Cut fish figures and a Jonah figure from plastic lids. The figures need to fit into the bottle opening. Use permanent markers to decorate the fish and Jonah.

Next have kids roll aluminum foil into balls and other shapes. Place these shapes and seashells in the water. Use glue and tape to secure the bottle top. Roll or shake the bottle on its side to see a raging sea with Jonah swimming for his life.

Paraphrase the story from **Jonah 1:1-14.** Ask: How do you think Jonah felt when he was thrown into the water? What would you have prayed if you had been Jonah? Have you ever been in a hopeless situation and tried praying about it? Explain. How did God answer your prayer?

LAST DAYS JOURNAL

Kids make journals to learn about some of the events in Jesus' last week.

WHAT YOU'LL NEED:

You'll need copy paper, construction paper, stapler, markers, and crayons.

FOR EXTRA IMPACT:

- Let kids form small groups to share their favorite entry from their journal.

- Let kids also make a family journal. Family members can take turns writing entries in it at home.

- Include blank pages in the journal, and encourage kids to continue to write and draw in their journals after Easter.

DIRECTIONS

Print the following entries and Scripture references on separate pages.

Sunday—Entering Jerusalem (Mark 11:1-10)

Monday—Judas' plot against Jesus (Matthew 26:1-16)

Tuesday—Last Supper (Matthew 26:26-30)

Wednesday—Gethsemane (Matthew 26:36-46); Betrayed and arrested (Luke 22:47-65)

Thursday—Tried by Jewish authorities (Matthew 27:11-31); Tried by Pilate (John 19:1-16)

Friday—Crucifixion (Matthew 27:32-54); Burial (Matthew 27:57-61)

Saturday—Guarding the tomb (Matthew 27:62-66)

Sunday—Empty tomb (Matthew 28:1-8); Appearing to disciples (Luke 24:36-48)

Photocopy enough pages for each child to have a complete set. Make journals by stapling a set of pages between two sheets of construction paper. Kids can decorate their journal covers.

Have kids take their journals home and read the Scriptures with their families on the appropriate day during the week before Easter.

MYSTERY CROSS

Kids learn about God's forgiveness.

WHAT YOU'LL NEED:

You'll need red plastic film, scissors, a red pencil, a lead pencil, and white paper.

FOR EXTRA IMPACT:

- Read aloud **Ephesians 1:7.** Have kids write on the white papers above the cross, "God forgives my sins."

- Ask kids what it means to them that God forgives their sins.

- Have kids sit in silence and think of something they've done that they want God to forgive. Then close in prayer with everyone saying aloud, "God forgive us for our sins."

DIRECTIONS

Have kids cut the film into the shape of a cross. Have them use the red pencil to write "sin" on white paper and then write "forgiveness" in lead pencil. Make sure the words fit within the borders of the cross.

Next have kids cover *forgiveness* with red pencil dots or scribbles so the word can't be easily read. Have kids slide the red film over the paper and watch "sin" disappear and "forgiveness" shine through.

Explain to children how Jesus died to take our sin away and replace it with God's forgiveness.

NATIVITY ORNAMENT

Kids make this aromatic crèche ornament to celebrate Christmas.

WHAT YOU'LL NEED:

You'll need a 6-inch length of ribbon, 5 cinnamon sticks, and a small wooden or cardboard star for each child. You'll also need yellow paint, paintbrushes, glitter, Christmas cards with Nativity scenes or a Nativity scene rubber stamp, colored pencils and paper, scissors, potpourri, and glue.

FOR EXTRA IMPACT:

- Bring in different crèche sets for children to see.

- Let kids create a crèche scene in the room using boxes, dolls, stuffed animals, and other props.

- Read aloud **Luke 2:4-7,** and have kids tell how Joseph and Mary might've felt when there was no room in the inn.

DIRECTIONS

Have kids each paint a small wooden star with yellow paint and sprinkle glitter over the wet paint. Allow the paint to dry. Glue five cinnamon sticks into the shape of a house.

As the glue on the house dries, create a Nativity scene by cutting out the Nativity figures on a Christmas card, drawing the figures on paper, or cutting out a rubber stamped Nativity scene on a sheet of paper. Glue the Nativity scene to the dried cinnamon-stick stable.

Glue potpourri onto the sides of the stable for a rustic look—and nice smell. Then glue the star to the top of the stable. Insert a 6-inch piece of ribbon through the top of the stable, and tie the ribbon to serve as a hanger.

ON MY HEART NECKLACE

Kids learn about keeping God's word close to their hearts.

WHAT YOU'LL NEED:

You'll need clay that hardens, a pencil, yarn, and markers.

FOR EXTRA IMPACT:

- Read aloud **Psalm 119:11.** Ask kids what it means to hide God's Word in their hearts.

- Make a list of ways we can keep God's Word in our hearts. Challenge kids to pick one thing from that list to do during the week.

- Let kids make an extra necklace for a friend. Wrap it in tissue paper, tie with yarn, and attach a tag with the words of **Psalm 119:11.**

DIRECTIONS

Have kids each make a necklace as a reminder to keep God's teachings close to their hearts. Have kids mold the clay into heart shapes. Or roll out the clay and cut out a heart shape using a cookie cutter. Help kids use a pencil to pierce an opening through the top of their hearts and to carve "God's Word" onto their hearts. Then let the clay harden according to package directions.

When the clay is ready, have kids decorate their hearts with markers. Thread and knot the yarn for the necklace "chain."

PEACEFUL MAGNETISM

Kids make refrigerator magnets to learn about peace.

WHAT YOU'LL NEED:

You'll need a roll of ½-inch flexible magnetic tape, 3 yellow 9x12-inch craft foam sheets, pencil, ruler, scissors, and puffy fabric paint.

FOR EXTRA IMPACT:

- Have kids write the words to the acrostic on a sheet of construction paper and decorate with markers. Kids can hang the reminder on their refrigerator with their letter magnets.

- Have kids tell ways we can be Christ's example to others.

- Read aloud **2 Corinthians 5:20,** and have kids tell why it's important for us to be Christ's ambassadors of peace to the world.

DIRECTIONS

Have kids cut each foam sheet in half to create two 6x9-inch sheets. Using a ruler as a guide, lightly draw large block letters on the foam sheets so that the letters spell "peace." Cut out the letters, and have kids decorate the front of the letters with fabric paint. Once the paint is dry, peel and place the adhesive side of the magnetic strip on the back of the letters.

Teach kids this acrostic for the letters: People Everywhere Acting out Christ's Example. Have kids take their letters home to hang on their refrigerators.

PILLOW PRESENTS

Older kids can help with the babies and toddlers in your nursery to make special gifts for others.

WHAT YOU'LL NEED:

You'll need washed and ironed plain pillowcases, fabric paint, pie tins, fabric markers, cardboard, and baby wipes.

FOR EXTRA IMPACT:

- Let older kids make their own pillowcase keepsakes. Have kids make handprints and footprints on a pillow case and then use a paint pen to write, "My hands and feet serve God."

- Have kids share ways they can use their hands and feet to serve God.

- Read aloud **Psalm 119:105**, and have kids tell ways God's Word is a lamp to our feet.

DIRECTIONS

Let older kids go to the nursery and help with the babies and toddlers to create precious presents that'll be treasured for years to come. Have each child make a Pillow Present with one of the babies or toddlers or have kids work in pairs.

Have kids each place cardboard in their pillowcase, then help pull off the baby's socks and shoes. Then dip the bottom of one foot into paint and press the painted foot onto the pillow case, keeping the cardboard under the area where you're painting. Do this several times to create a baby-foot border on the pillowcase. With toddlers, you can use their footprints or handprints. Use baby wipes to wash off feet and hands.

Once the border is created, have kids write a message in the center of the pillowcase, then give the gift pillowcase away. Suggested gift ideas:

For nursing home residents, "God's Word is a light unto your feet!"

For new mothers, "Welcome! From your pals at the First Church!" Fill the pillowcase with baby gifts and deliver to Mom at a baby shower or the hospital.

For nursery volunteers, teachers, the children's director, or the senior pastor, "Thanks for teaching us to walk in the ways of Jesus!"

POINTED REMINDER

Kids make these cross necklaces as a reminder of Jesus' sacrifice.

WHAT YOU'LL NEED:

You'll need a Bible, long and short nails, fine-gauge wire, and nylon cord.

FOR EXTRA IMPACT:

- Ask kids: How does it feel to know that Christ died for your sins? Explain.

- Encourage kids to each hold their cross and think about their sins that Jesus died for. Close with each child offering a prayer of thanks to Jesus.

- Let kids make extra necklaces to share Jesus' love with others.

DIRECTIONS

Say: For Christians, Good Friday is the most solemn day of the year because it's the day we remember the suffering and death of Jesus. Read aloud **Matthew 27:33-50**. Say: Jesus died for us so we can have eternal life. To help us remember Christ's death for us, let's make a cross necklace.

Give each child four nails, two of which are a little shorter than the other two. Lay the two long nails head to point next to each other. Similarly, lay the two shorter ones across the long nails to form a cross. Bind them together with fine-gauge wire, and suspend the cross on a nylon cord to make a necklace. Have kids wear their necklaces as a reminder of Jesus' sacrifice for us.

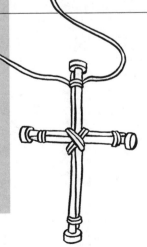

UPPER ELEMENTARY

PRAISE PINWHEELS

Kids tell others about Jesus with these fun conversation starters.

WHAT YOU'LL NEED:

You'll need construction paper, scissors, straight pins, beads, and pencils.

FOR EXTRA IMPACT:

- Read aloud **Psalm 9:1,** and have kids tell wonderful things God has done in their lives.

- Teach kids the words to this rhyming prayer:

  I praise you, God, with all my heart, for all that you have done.

  I sing your praises here and there as I tell everyone.

- Have kids write the words of **Psalm 9:1** on a tag and attach it to their pinwheel with string as a reminder to praise the Lord.

DIRECTIONS

Give each child a sheet of construction paper and scissors. Have kids cut off 2½ inches from the short side of the paper. Have kids cut the paper from each corner toward the center, leaving about ½ inch uncut in the middle. Pull every other outer point into the middle and push a straight pin through the center to hold the paper points in the middle. Put a bead on the pin behind the paper wheel, then push the pin into the eraser on a long pencil.

Say: One of the most exciting parts about knowing Jesus is being able to tell others about him. Who can you tell about Jesus? Suggest that children give their pinwheels to these people as a way of starting up a conversation about Jesus.

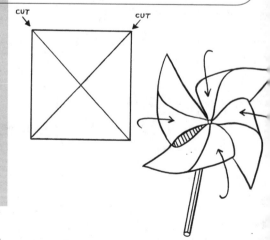

RAIN STICK

Kids love these gentle noisemakers.

WHAT YOU'LL NEED:

For each rain stick, you'll need 1 empty paper-towel tube, 20 finishing nails, ⅓ cup dry rice, glue, masking tape, and a Bible. You'll also need craft materials such as tempera paint, craft beads, feathers, and glitter.

FOR EXTRA IMPACT:

- Have kids take turns telling promises they've made to others and how it feels when people keep their promises.

- For a quick craft, pre-prepare each rain stick tube by using a piece of aluminum foil about one and half times the length of your tube and about 6 inches wide. Crunch the aluminum foil into two long, thin, snake-like shapes, and then twist each one into a spring shape and place in the tube.

- Kids can choose a favorite song and together use their rain sticks as accompaniment instruments.

DIRECTIONS

Have kids press the nails through the spiral seam of the cardboard paper towel roll about 2 inches apart. Apply a dot of glue to each nail to hold it in place. When the glue has dried, cover one end of the roll with masking tape. Pour the rice in the tube. Cover the open end and secure it with masking tape.

Read aloud **Genesis 9:16.** Say, "After God sent rains that flooded the earth, he promised to never again flood the earth. God created a rainbow so that whenever we see one, we'll remember God's promise."

Have kids use the craft materials to decorate their rain sticks with rainbows to remind them of God's promise in **Genesis 9:16.**

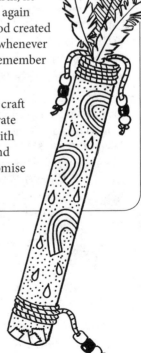

SPLATTER PRINTS

Kids will learn that God can transform bad situations into something good.

WHAT YOU'LL NEED:

You'll need a Bible, salad spinner, paper, scissors, tempera paint, and paintbrushes.

FOR EXTRA IMPACT:

- If you don't have a salad spinner, use a shallow cardboard box. Have kids place paper inside the box, drop splatters of paint on the paper, and roll marbles on the paper.

- Fill plastic cups one quarter full of unpopped popcorn and stir in one spoonful of paint. Place one sheet of paper in the bottom of a shallow box, pour the paint-coated kernels onto the paper, and shake the box gently to create a design.

DIRECTIONS

One at a time, have kids cut a long, rectangular strip of paper and place it around the edge inside the salad-spinner basket. Then place dabs of paint on the paper, close the lid, and turn the handle. Open the spinner, take out the beautiful picture, and show it to the group. Set aside to dry.

Ask: Which picture do you like the best—the one before or after it was changed? Explain.

Share with kids a situation God transformed in your life. Then say: Tell about a bad thing that has happened to you or someone you know. How did God turn that bad thing into something good? Did you learn a big lesson through it? Explain.

Read aloud **Romans 8:28.** Say: The Bible says God can take the bad things in our lives and transform them into something good. God does this for us because he loves us and wants us to become more like Christ. Let's pray and thank God for the good he brings out of bad things.

SUMMER REPORTS

Kids celebrate all the great things that happened during the summer with this creative idea.

WHAT YOU'LL NEED:

You'll need a medium-size box and lid for each child, old magazines and catalogs, construction paper, fine-tip markers, scissors, and Mod-Podge decoupage glue.

FOR EXTRA IMPACT:

- Take a photo of each child. Have kids each glue their photo onto their box lid with Mod Podge for a fun visible reminder of how they're changing throughout the year.

- Write a note of encouragement to each child to put in his or her box.

- Let kids work together to make a classroom collage box for a fun time capsule. Put in a class photo and add other mementos throughout the year to enjoy viewing at year's end.

DIRECTIONS

Lay out old magazines and catalogs, and have kids cut out or write phrases or words on construction paper that describe things they did during the summer, such as vacation, swimming, or reading. Then have them cut out pictures that show the things they did. Have kids glue these images to their boxes using Mod-Podge.

As their collage boxes are drying, have kids take turns describing their creations and their summer activities. Then encourage them to take their boxes home and use them to store new school memories, such as favorite notes, crafts, or valentines.

At the end of the school year, have kids bring their boxes back to church and share their memories.

UNMASKED

Kids explore how to be honest with others.

WHAT YOU'LL NEED:

You'll need a Bible, 8½x11 pieces of cardboard, scissors, pencils, feathers, yarn, tinsel, chenille wires, paint, paintbrushes, glue, elastic, and a stapler.

FOR EXTRA IMPACT:

- Let kids have a fashion show and take turns modeling their mask creations.

- Have kid hang their masks on a bulletin board and write the caption: "Don't hide behind a mask...instead, in God's light shall you bask!"

- Have kids share things that make them afraid and want to hide behind a mask. Remind kids that God sees our hearts and we have nothing to fear with him.

▶ DIRECTIONS

Have kids each cut their cardboard into any shape they want to make their mask. Cut out the eyeholes and decorate the mask using the craft materials. Have kids measure out a length of elastic that will fit around their heads. Staple the elastic piece to each side of the mask. Have kids wear their masks.

Ask: Why do people wear masks? What purpose does a mask serve? What kind of imaginary masks can people wear to hide who they really are? What do you think God thinks of people wearing these imaginary masks?

Read aloud **1 John 1:5-7.** Ask: How is wearing a mask like walking in the darkness? What does it mean to walk in the light? Why do some people try to hide who they are by walking in the darkness? How can we be more honest with each other? How can we continue to walk in the light?

Close in prayer asking for God's help to walk in the light and be honest with each other.

OLD TESTAMENT

INDEX

NEW TESTAMENT

INDEX

INDEX

SEASONAL INDEX

INDEX